Also by Dave Ho]

Novels

The Shed

- A disgruntled guy takes time out in a moorland monastery, crossing paths with rock stars, wanderers, world-changers and of course… monks

Dead Prophets Society

- A town turned upside-down by a gang of revolutionary punks

Sons of Thunder

- A contemporary gospel, the Messiah in Cornwall with surfers and mechanics for disciples

No More Heroes

- Cain, Solomon & Jacob in a modern tale of men, women, dads and crime

Other

Top Stories

- 31 parables retold with serious and humorous contemporary comments

Pulp Gospel

- 31 bits of the Bible retold with gritty reflections and comments

Rebel Yell: 31 Psalms

- Psalms, God & Rock'n'Roll

Faith & Film

- Movie clips that bring the Bible to life

The Bloke's Bible

- Bits of the Bible retold for guys

The Bloke's Bible 2: The Road Trip

- More Bible bits retold

For more information visit Dave's website – davehopwood.com

Telling Tales

INTRODUCTION

Response stories are pieces which involve the whole audience (and the whole family); they are dramatic stories which can be used with little rehearsal or preparation. Each story contains 4 to 8 key words or phrases which are repeated at different points throughout the story. Whenever the audience or congregation hear the key words they should respond with the appropriate noise or action. The story can be delivered by a narrator alone or a whole group may lead the responses from the front - such a group may be rehearsed or spontaneous. You may like to write down the responses on large cards which the group hold up whenever each key word occurs.

It is important when telling the story to adopt a fairly animated style, and don't be afraid to stop and encourage the audience if they start flagging. The material for some of the stories has been lifted straight from the Bible as in *David the Giant-Killer*; in others the material has been modernised as in the case of *David and Goliath*. Before beginning the story take time to explain all the key words and responses clearly, as it can be frustrating for both the narrator and the audience if folks long to join in but haven't quite grasped the whole picture.

This book contains 135 of these pieces previously published in three books - *Telling Tales, Telling More Tales* and *Telling Even More Tales*. But other similar sketches can easily be created. Why not have a go yourself? Any Bible story, parable, or theme can be brought to life and understood with this simple style of presentation. The key words need to occur frequently enough to keep the attention of the audience - but not so often that they become boring. It may also be helpful if 1 or 2 of the words relate in some way to the point of the story, as it is these words that the audience is most likely to remember afterwards. To engage parts of the audience in competition with each other is a good tool: e.g. Who can make the most noise?!

So - got the idea? Why not give it a try? These stories are excellent material for family services, school assemblies, or Sunday schools - and they are also good "up the sleeve" routines for unexpected situations! Also, any of the pieces contained within this book may be used simply as straight stories without audience participation.

No licence need be obtained however they are used.

Note on stage directions. The stage directions given for each response are extremely brief. Usually if they are in speech marks then the audience should say these lines, e.g. in *The Jonah Factor*, **Star** - "Thank you, fans! Thank you, fans!" You might like to embellish these, e.g. flicking back your hair in true pop star fashion as you say them. Sometimes a general phrase is used to describe the response, as in *Mary and the angel*, **Wedding** - Wedding bells. This is to suggest that the audience should make this noise, or mime pulling on bell ropes, or both (You decide which is best). Often I have left it to your discretion as to how you use the responses. Also in *Mary and the angel* you will find the response **Kitchen** - Kitchen sounds. You may like to divide the audience into sections and give each section a specific noise to make, like a tap running, a washing machine humming, a coffee percolator bubbling, or vegetables being chopped. Or you may ask everyone to do exactly the same noise, or you may ask everyone to make their own noise. Having said this, it is always helpful to suggest and demonstrate the responses, to give the audience the right idea. If you simply ask them to make kitchen sounds they may have no idea what to do and may subsequently sit quietly in their seats for the duration of the story! Leading by example is the best way to encourage an enthusiastic response. Try and be as animated as you can as you teach the responses and tell the story.

INDEX

Other Stories

Psalm of Creation

Rain - "Spitter spatter!" **Eat** - Chewing noises **Planted** - Dig hole
Made - Mix cement with appropriate noises
Trees - Hold up arms, finger splayed
Earth - Rub fingers together **Hunting** - Throw spear/Fire arrow

Many of these stories take a contemporary angle in some of the responses. For example, in this story whenever the word *Made* is mentioned everyone should pretend to mix cement, as if about to build a house or a wall. This is a deliberate ploy to help the children to think about these stories in a way which they can relate to, of course it is highly unlikely that God did use sand and cement when he set to work on this planet - but who knows!

When God **made** everything, he took the heavens and spread them out like a very big tent. Then he rode around the **earth** on top of the clouds as if they were a white chariot. He made springs begin to flow in the valleys, and rivers in the hills. He watched as the animals came to the water to drink when they were thirsty, and nearby, in the trees that God had **planted**, the birds began to sing. He **made rain** and dropped it from the sky, and it helped the **earth** and **made** things grow. There was grass for the cows to **eat**, and plants and vegetables for the people. Crops began to grow, and the people **made** lovely fresh bread from the corn, and wine from the grapes. The tall **trees** on the mountains got plenty of **rain** as well, God was proud of those **trees**, he **planted** them himself. The birds came and made nests in the **trees** and wild goats lived in the mountains and badgers in the cliffs.

God **made** the sun and moon to show us day and night, and each new month as it came around. He **made** the night, and that was the time that lots of the animals went **hunting** for food to **eat**. The lions went out **hunting** and roared with all their might as they looked for food to **eat** which God had provided, but when the sun came up they stopped **hunting** and went back to their dens to sleep, while all the people got up and went to work.

The **earth** is crammed full of animals that God has **made**, and the sea is full of fish and creatures - there are too many of them to ever count. He sends **rain** to give us all food to **eat**, and to water the **trees** he has **planted**.

He has **made** so many things and we all depend on him. Let us always remember that the **earth** is God's - and let's thank him for everything he has made.

Adam and Eve

Fruit/Vegetables - Lick lips   **Flowers** - Smell flowers
Garden/Tree - Gentle breeze in the trees

Or you may like to get the audience to create the sounds of a luxurious garden with their eyes shut, whilst you tell the whole story. You could divide them into sections and ask one section to be the sound of the wind blowing gently through the garden, another section to be the birds, another to be the sound of grasshoppers, another to be the rustling of the leaves on the trees. If they do this get them all to fade the noise down towards the end so that it is silent during the last paragraph.

It was a very beautiful **garden**. The **trees** were heavy with ripe **fruit**, the air was rich with the scent of sweet **flowers**, and everywhere the soil was loaded with herbs and **vegetables**. Adam stretched his tanned arms and leant back against the **tree** to reflect upon the day. It had been as busy as ever, watching the animals at play in the morning, and poetry to compose in the afternoon. Tomorrow he might invent a new sport, or else go exploring over the far side of the **garden**.

That was the moment he turned his head and caught sight of her - Eve making her careful way through the orchard towards him. She smiled and he returned her gaze, though she seemed different that evening. She had had a good day she said, and presented him with a basket of beautiful **flowers**, still full in bloom. Nestled in the centre there was a piece of **fruit**.

Adam knew instantly what it was. But he still questioned her. Yes, she told him, it had come from that **tree**, the one they had been warned about. Yes, she knew the consequences of tasting that **fruit**, she knew they might die. Then she smiled and spoke.
"But I'm not dead, am I?"

That was the moment the truth dawned. So that was the difference he noticed. He despised and envied her in the same moment. Her long fingers plucked the **fruit** from it's nest in the basket and placed it on his palm.

It had been a very beautiful **garden**. The **trees** once heavy with ripe **fruit**, now stooped a little, and the scent of the sweet **flowers** seemed no longer rich. Everywhere the soil was loaded with herbs and **vegetables**... and weeds. Adam stretched his tired arms and leant back against the **tree** to recover from the day. It had been as busy as ever, working the ground in the morning, and clothes to repair in the afternoon. Tomorrow he might make a new shovel, if he had the time.

Shame about the argument with Eve that morning, he seemed to recall a day when they hadn't bothered with such things. A piece of **fruit** fell from the **tree** into the dead leaves at his feet, wearily he reached over and took it, a whisper of guilt played somewhere in the back of his mind...

Mr Noah and the Great Flood

by Fiona Stewart-Darling

Sawing - Sawing action and sound   **Hammering** - "Bang! Bang!"
Tired - Yawn   **Painting** - Brush strokes action   **Flood** - Hands rise up
Animals - Appropriate noises   **Raining** - Fingers make falling rain

Mr Noah was six hundred years old, he and his family had always prayed to God and trusted Him. One day God had a serious talk with Mr Noah. "It makes me very sad that all the people are spoiling the world, they are cruel and unkind to each other. I will have to start all over again."
Mr Noah was very upset when he heard God say this, but he had to admit that God was right.
"What are you going to do, God?" he asked.
God said to Mr Noah, "I want you to build an Ark (which is a very large boat), build it big enough for you and all your family and for two of every kind of **animal**, every kind of **bird** and every **creepy crawly**, because I am going to send a huge thunder storm and it is going to **rain** so hard that there will be a **flood**."

So Mr Noah with the help of his sons Ham, Shem and Japheth built a huge big Ark in his back garden. There was lots of **sawing**, lots of **hammering** and lots of **painting**. This went on day after day, more **sawing**, more **hammering** and more **painting**. Mr Noah's friends thought he was very silly and they would not listen to him because they did not believe in God.
But Mr Noah and his sons continued **sawing** and **hammering** and **painting**, until one day the Ark was at last finished.

The next thing Mr Noah had to do was to find all the **animals**, **birds** and **creepy crawlies**. He had two of every kind. There were two **elephants**, two **lions**, two **monkeys**, two **pigs**, two **cows**, two **ducks**, two **birds**, two **bees** and two **spiders**. What other animals do you think came along too? [Give the audience a chance to name other animals and do appropriate actions and sounds.]

Then - it began **raining**. It **rained** and it **rained** and it **rained** and it **rained**. The **floods** came up and up and up... and kept on coming up for forty days and forty nights. [Get everyone to **count from 1 to 40**.] Soon all the trees, all the houses and all the buildings were under water. All that Mr Noah could see was water, water and more water. Then they realised it had gone very quiet outside... it had stopped **raining**. The sun had come out and it was getting very hot. Soon the **floods** started to go down and so Mr Noah sent out one of the **birds** to look for dry land, and at tea time it came back looking very **tired** - but in its beak it had some leaves... the bird had found some dry ground.

The next day the Ark suddenly stopped because the ground was dry again. So God told Mr Noah to open the doors and let out all the **animals**, **birds** and **creepy crawlies**. So out they all went. And God promised that He would never let it rain so much again, and to remind us of this He put a rainbow in the sky so that every time we see it we can think of God and remember His promises.

Noah and the Ark

Any insect - Crawling fingers on person near you   **Sleezy -** Shocked
People - "Rhubarb, rhubarb, rhubarb!"   **Rain** - Tap fingers
Boat - "Chug chug!"   **Any animal** - Appropriate sound
Big & Wide - Hold out arms to show size   **Float** - "Glug glug!"

Alternatively - You may like to deliver this as a rap. Get the audience to
click to a rhythm, and one or two readers then read the story in time. You
may need to adapt the script slightly for this! And you need to deliver it
with confidence.

"Hey Noah!" said God,
"I know it sounds odd,
But I want you to build a **boat**.
I want it just this **big**,
And just this **wide**,
And make sure it can **float**!"

"I'm not too pleased
About the **sleezy**
Things I see down there.
All the **people** hate each other
And no one seems to care."

"I'll make it plain -
It's going to **rain**.
Hang   on, I've not finished yet!
You and your folks will be alright -
But the **people** will all get wet!"

"When the **rain** starts coming
Just start running
And leap aboard the **boat**,
Take all the **animals** with you
And take a good strong coat."

"Take lots of **bugs**,
And **snails** and **slugs**,
Monkeys, **dogs** and **cats**,
Spiders, **creepy crawlies**,
And lots of **vampire bats**!"

"No, wait a minute,
There won't be room in it!
Just two of each for a start.
Two **mice**, two **rats**, two **hamsters**,
And keep the **rabbits** well apart!"

"When the **rain's** come down
And the **people** have drowned
It will be such a shame.
But at least the world will have had a good wash
And we can all start again."

"So listen, son,
This must be done,
It's no use you complainin'.
Just get a brolly, build that **boat**,
And I'll see you when it stops **raining**."

Joseph's Dream

Forgot/Forget - "Uhh..."   **Brothers** - "Oh oh!"   **Dreams** - "Wow!"
Prison - "Clang!"   **Egypt** - Sand dance   **Coat** - "Zzzzzippp!"
Kiss - Kissing noise   **Idea** - "Ding!" Hold up finger
Prime Minister - Wave   **Potty** - "Clang!"

Joseph had a cool **coat** and eleven **brothers** - so the house was a bit of a squash. They all had long names and he often used to **forget** them and mix them up. So he called his **brothers** - (Count on fingers) Rube, Sim, Lev, Jude, Iss, Zeb, Ben, Dan, Gad, Ash and Naff - for short. They called him a pain! Partly because he kept **forgetting** their names, and partly because he had really wild **dreams**. He **dreamt** about everything - lions, marmite, gladiators, stars, shredded wheat and even a pig called Babe!
He always told his **brothers** about the **dreams** - and they told him about their **dream** - which was to get rid of Joseph - forever!

One night Joseph **dreamt** that he was in charge of all his **brothers**, a bit like being the **prime minister**. He thought the **dream** was a great **idea**, so he told his **brothers**, and they had a great **idea**. They took Joseph out in the desert and dropped him into a hole, then they ran off. Later they came back and said sorry, then they sold him as a slave to some people from **Egypt**.

In **Egypt** Joseph ended up in a really big house. The owner was called Potiphar - but Joseph soon   shortened it to **Potty**, so he wouldn't **forget** it. **Potty**'s wife was very beautiful, and one day she tried to **kiss** Joseph, so he panicked and jumped out of the window, leaving his **coat** behind. Luckily the window was on the ground floor - but unluckily he landed on top of **Potty** who was so angry he flung him into **prison**.
Well, it's a very long story - but in the end God got Joseph out of **prison**, he met the King of **Egypt**, became **Prime Minister**, and was put in charge of everyone - including his **brothers**, which was exactly what was in his **dream**.

Moses and Pharaoh

No! - Whine: "Ohh!" **Blood** - "Ugh!" **Jump** - "Boiing!"
Hail - Flick face and say: "Ouch!" **Gnats/Flies** - Buzzing
Die - Hands to mouth, looking shocked **Pharaoh** - Bow

"Can we leave Egypt," Moses said, "that's all we want to do?
And if we go, please **Pharaoh**, we'll be no trouble for you."

"**No!**" said **Pharaoh**, "you cannot go, 'cause I'm in charge round here!
I'm the one who says what goes - and you lot don't - d'you hear?"

"Well, **Pharaoh** listen, it's Moses here, we've really got to go,
God's told me that if we don't there'll be a lot of trouble you know.

First the Nile will turn to **blood**, then the frogs will **jump**,
Then the **gnats** will drive you mad, and **flies** give you the hump.

Then all the animals will **die**, and you'll get boils in nasty places;
It'll **hail**, and the locusts' come - and wipe the smile right off your faces.

Then the sun will disappear, and worst of all your child might **die**.
It all seems quite unnecessary if you'll just let us say goodbye?"

"**No!**" said **Pharaoh**, "**No**, **no**, **no**! The answer's really **no**.
There'll be no one to do my work if I let you lot go."

Moses bowed his weary head, it really seemed a shame,
But God had told him what would come, and it could not be changed.

When Moses had been born he had been hidden in the river,
'Til **Pharaoh's** daughter came along, and thought she heard him shiver.

They took him home and he'd been raised as if he was a prince,
But Moses killed a man one day, he'd never been the same since.

God had met him in the desert and told him what to do
Moses hadn't been so keen - but God had helped him through.

So here he stood in front of **Pharaoh**, "Let my people go!"
He pleaded time and time again - but **Pharaoh** still said... "**No!**"

Joshua and the Big Walls

Six days - Recite: "Monday, Tuesday, Wednesday, Thursday, Friday, Saturday."
Trumpets - Make trumpet noise, or use kazoos or other whistles
Shout - "Oi!"   **Walls** - Mime putting hands on invisible wall
N.B. The secret with this is to always press your hand against your invisible wall, not just to place it. So begin with one hand curved then press it flat as you put it against your invisible wall. The other rule is never to move both hands at once. Leave one hand on the wall while you move the other one. That way the wall never disappears and you and the audience can always see where it is.
Seven/Seventh - All count: "One two three four five six seven"
Sword - Mime swinging a sword, making appropriate noise
Crashing down - Shout "Crash!"

This story incorporates reciting the days of the week and counting from one to seven. Similarly, *Noah and the Great Flood* involves counting from one to forty. These stories can be an educational tool if the responses involve reciting these kind of things... months of the year, different colours, the alphabet, boys or girls names, books of the Bible and so on.

One day, while Joshua was leading the people of Israel on a journey across the desert, they came to a city with some very big **walls**.
While Joshua was looking at these **walls** he bumped into a man who was holding a **sword**. The man was sent by God and he told Joshua what to do next.

Joshua and his men had to march around the city for **six days**, carrying their **trumpets**.
Then on the **seventh day** they were to march around **seven times**, blowing their **trumpets**. Then after one long blast on the **trumpets**, all the men had to **shout**, and those huge **walls**, would come **crashing down**.

So Joshua went back to his people and told them what the man with the **sword** had said. And for **six days** they marched round and round the city, and on the **seventh day** they went round **seven times**, blew their **trumpets** and gave a massive **shout**. And then they had to dive out of the way because those huge **walls** came **crashing down**.

20
Gideon

Midianites - "Boo!"   **Fleece** - "Baa!"
Winepress - "Squelch squelch!" **Angel** - "Flap flap!"
Frightened - Bite nails   **Gideon** - "Who, me?"

There was once a young man called **Gideon**. Yes. And **Gideon** - oh yes, he worked in a **winepress**. He wasn't very brave, in fact most of the time he was **frightened** - because he was the smallest person in his family. One day while he was in the **winepress** he saw an **angel** who said to him: "Hello **Gideon**!" "Yes you!" said the **angel**. "I've got a job for you." "But I've already got one - in this **winepress**." said **Gideon**, and he was now very **frightened**.
The **angel** said: "Now listen **Gideon** - yes you! I want you to go and fight the **Midianites**."
"The... the... the... **Midianites**!" said **Gideon**. "Yes - YOU!!"
"But the reason I'm in this **winepress** is to get away from the **Midianites**. I mean the **Midianites** are big... and bad. And I'm **frightened**!"
"No need to be," said the **angel**, "God will help you, **Gideon**." "Yes - you."

Then he had an idea. "I've got this **fleece**," he said to the **angel**, "if I put it on the ground can God make the **fleece** wet, but leave the ground dry? If he does that I'll know he can help me."
So he laid out the **fleece** and went to bed. And in the morning - God had done it. The **fleece** was soaking wet - and **Gideon** - that's the one - was very **frightened**. So **frightened** that he made God do the **fleece** trick all over again.

But eventually **Gideon** - yup - obeyed the **angel**, left the **winepress** and even though he was small and **frightened**,   with just a few other men he defeated a whole army of **Midianites** because he trusted God, and God helped him.

Samson and Delilah

Strong - "Huh!" and flex muscles   **No** - Shake head
In love - "Aaah!"   **Enemies** - "Boo!" Thumbs down
Nagged - Make yapping mouths with hands
Shouted - "Look out - it's the bad guys!"   **Hair** - Snip snip!

Samson was the **strongest** man that ever lived. Before he was born an angel appeared from heaven to tell his parents that he must only eat and drink certain things, and that they must never cut his **hair**.

Well, Samson grew up to be very **strong** - so **strong** that he could fight lions with his bare hands and so **strong** that he could take on thirty of his **enemies** all at once - and win. He would have been very good at world wrestling.

One day he met a woman called Delilah and he fell **in love** with her. She was very beautiful, but she wasn't **in love** with him. Samson's **enemies** went to Delilah and asked her to find out just what made Samson so **strong**, because his **enemies** wanted to kill him.

So one day, while they were having some tea, Delilah said:
"Why are you so **strong**, Samson? Is it all those exercises you do?"
"**No**." said Samson.
"Is it all that Marmite you eat, then?"
"**No**."
"Is it all that wrestling you watch?"
"**No**."
Well, Delilah **nagged** him for a long time, and eventually, because he was **in love**, he told her that if he was tied up with special ropes, then he would lose all his strength, and become like Mr Bean!
So while he was asleep Delilah tiptoed up to him and tied him up with the special ropes. Then she **shouted**: "*Look out - it's the bad guys!*"
Samson woke up, ripped off the ropes and escaped, as **strong** as ever.
Next day, Delilah asked him again:
"What makes you so **strong**?"

Samson told her that if his **hair** was tied back he wouldn't be able to do anything. So when he fell asleep, Delilah tied it up. Then she **shouted**: "...."
Samson woke up and ran off.

Now Delilah was very unhappy, because she knew he hadn't told her the truth. So she **nagged**, and **nagged**, and **nagged**, and **nagged** until eventually he told her. He had never cut his **hair** and that's why he was so **strong**. So this time Delilah made him fall asleep then his **enemies** cut off all his **hair**, and when she **shouted**: "...." He lost all his strength and couldn't run away. Then they took Samson to the temple and chained him up in between two very large pillars.

Samson was very sad, because he shouldn't have told anyone about his **hair**, but he decided to ask for God's help. So he prayed that God would make him **strong** just one more time so that he could fight against all his **enemies**. And suddenly, he flexed his muscles, threw back his head and ripped the chains off his arms. Then, **strong** as ever, he pushed the two concrete pillars over and the whole roof caved in, crushing all of Samson's **enemies** in one go.

Ruth's Best Friend

Friends - Give each other a *high five*
Home - Watch TV and have a drink
No - All shake heads vigorously   **Yes** - All nod vigorously
Difficult - Look worried and shocked
Eat - Mime eating with plenty of noise

Ruth and Noami were very good **friends**. They lived in a place called
Moab. One day Naomi said to Ruth, "It's time for me to go back **home**, to
the place where I was born."
Ruth wanted to go with her because they were such good **friends**, but
Naomi said, "**No**" she couldn't go with her.
"Please," Ruth begged, "let me come with you."
"**No**," said Naomi. "This is your **home**. You can't come."
"**Yes** I can - I want to come," said Ruth.
"**No**, you can't," said Naomi.
"**Yes** I can." said Ruth.
"**No** you can't." said Naomi.
"**Yes** I can."
"**No**."
"**Yes**."
This went on for quite some time.
"Why won't you stay here?" asked Naomi.
Ruth said, "Wherever you go - I want to go. Wherever you live - that'll be
my **home**. Whatever you **eat**, I'll **eat**, whatever you go through I'll go
through."
"It might be **difficult**," said Naomi.
"It might be **difficult**," said Ruth, "But we are **friends**, and I will stick by
you."
So they stayed together and Ruth went with Naomi.

David the Giant-Killer

by Fiona Stewart-Darling

Goliath - Boo and hiss   **Gasp** - Sharp intake of breath
Frightened - Bite nails   **Crashed** - Clap hands
Fight - Hold fists up   **David** - Clap/cheer/whistle

King Saul and the Israelites were at war with the Philistines. King Saul was a tall man; but **Goliath**, the Philistine champion, was a giant - almost 9 feet tall! He wore a great bronze helmet, carried a huge spear, and had a very heavy shield. Every day, morning and night, for forty days **Goliath** walked up and down in front of the Israelite army.

"I dare one of you to come out and **fight** me," he roared. "If he wins we will be your slaves. But if I win, you will be our slaves."

When King Saul and his soldiers saw him they just stood there and **gasped**. They were all too **frightened** to **fight**.

Then one day young **David** arrived with food for his brothers, who were soldiers. He was just a shepherd boy. **David** listened to **Goliath's** jeering words - wasn't anyone going to **fight** him?

King saul had offered a huge reward to the man who killed **Goliath**.

"He shall marry my daughter - the princess, and I will let his family off all taxes." But still no-one came forward.

"Who is this Philistine to defy the army of the living God?" **David** said. His brothers tried to shut him up - who did he think he was?

But someone told the king and he sent for **David**.

"Your majesty," **David** said, "no one should be **frightened** of this Philistine. I will go and **fight** him."

"How could you **fight** him?" Saul asked. "You are only a shepherd boy and **Goliath** has been a soldier all his life."

"I've killed lions and bears," **David** said, "when I looked after sheep. If God can save me from lions and bears he will certainly save me from **Goliath**."

"Very well," said Saul. "But you must wear my helmet and coat of armour."

David put it on, but he could hardly walk in it.

"I can't **fight** like this," he said. So he took it all off, picked up his shepherd's stick and chose five smooth, round stones from the stream for his sling.

Then he went to meet **Goliath**.

When **Goliath** saw **David** coming he threw back his head and roared with laughter. "Is this the best **fighter** the Israelites have? What's that stick for, boy? Do you think I'm a dog?"

"You have come to **fight** with your sword and spear," **David** said. "But I come in the name of the living God. He does not need swords and spears to save his people. Soon everyone will know that Israel has a God."

He ran towards **Goliath**, letting fly with his sling. The stone smashed into the giant's forehead and knocked him down. He **crashed** to the ground. Quick as lightning **David** ran to him, drew **Goliath's** sword and cut off his head.

There was a great **gasp** from the Philistine army. They turned and ran, with the Israelites in hot persuit. God had come and rescued his people. His people were safe - thanks to **David** the shepherd boy who dared to trust God.

David and Goliath

Sling - Swing imaginary sling   **Lion** - Roar   **Swooned** - Swoon
Sheep/shepherd - Bleat appropriate name e.g. "Baarney!" "Laambert" "Baarbara"
     Harp - "Twang!"   **Stone** - "Ouch!"   **Goliath** - "Grrrrr!"

You can always act out any of these stories, of course. I once saw a group present this one, with all the responses, but also demonstrating the story as it unfolded. So one person took the role of David, and another Goliath. This might work well in an assembly, asking volunteers to come up the front and take the different parts of the lion, Jesse, and the people in the town, as well as the two central characters.

Now David was a **shepherd** - a right plucky lad,
He weren't afraid of storms, or **lions**, or thieves or anything bad.
He often used to sit and watch the sun as it went down,
He'd play his **harp**, and sing his songs, as the **sheep** snored on the ground.

His father's name was Jesse, in all   he had eight sons,
But none of them was as bright or brave as David, the youngest one.
David had a secret weapon, he called it his **sling**,
And when a **lion** crept up on him - he'd hit it with the thing.

He'd put a **stone** in the pouch and swing it round his head,
He'd shout like Tarzan, run like mad, and kill that **lion** dead.
The **sheep** they rather liked him - they'd never had it so good;
Dynamic Dave they used to call him, well, I suppose they would.

Now this boy's finest hour came one Sunday afternoon,
When this huge great giant turned up - and all the women **swooned**.
They weren't alone, the men **swooned** too and scarpered pretty quick,
But when David heard about this man he wouldn't take no stick.

He grabbed his **sling**, and took his **harp**, and wandered into town.
The men were shaking in their boots, and hiding underground.
Goliath was the giant's name - he was an ugly brute,
Not like David - he was cool and the girls thought he was cute.

Well, they stood and stared out in the sun, it was just like *High Noon*,
And **Goliath** laughed when he saw this boy, and said "Give us a tune!"
He saw that David had his **harp**, and he thought he might just sing,
What he didn't see was his cunning plan, and his rather useful **sling**.

Goliath said he'd kill them all, cause he hated all the town,
David didn't say a word, he smiled, and just bent down.
Well **Goliath** ranted on and on - and everyone got bored,
David got down on his knees and had a word with the Lord.

The boy picked up five small **stones** and put one in his **sling**,
Then he swung it round and round his head and let fly with the thing.
Goliath tried to head it off - a silly move to make -
'cause the little **stone** it cracked his skull and didn't half give him a headache!

Well the folks went mad, **Goliath** dropped dead, and David said a prayer,
He knew that he could trust in God, he knew that He'd be there.
He grabbed his **sling**, and smiled at folks and strolled back to his **sheep**,
They didn't even know he'd gone - they were all still fast asleep.

Elijah and the Rain

Look - Mime looking through binoculars   **Sea** - Make sea noises
Mountain - Running feet, mountain shape with hands
Bushes - Say: "Rustle scratch, rustle scratch!"
Rocks - Say: "Stumble ouch, stumble ouch!"
Beach - Say "Shuffle shuffle!" and shuffle feet   **Rain** - Drum fingers

This piece was inspired by the old *bear hunt* story, where the reader takes the audience through a number of obstacles in order to reach the end of the trail. This works well if the narrator speeds up as the story progresses. So, the first time you take the audience "down the **mountain**, through the **bushes**, over the **rocks**, and down to the **beach**" you may like to read it quite slowly, leaving plenty of time for everyone to think, but by the end of the story you should be racing through this list of obstacles, particularly as Elijah and his servant end up running for safety themselves at the end of the adventure.

It hadn't **rained** for a long time and everywhere was very dry. Elijah was a prophet who had said this would happen, and he was right. But now he knew it was time for it to **rain** again. So he went up a **mountain** to pray. He bowed down low with his head between his knees.
He told his servant, "Go and **look** out to **sea**."

So the servant went down the **mountain**, through the **bushes**, over the **rocks**, down to the **beach** and there he **looked** out to **sea**. Then he went back to Elijah and said. "There's nothing there."
Elijah told him to go again. So the servant went down the **mountain**, through the **bushes**, over the **rocks**, down to the **beach** and there he **looked** out to **sea**.
Still there was nothing, so he went and told Elijah. Elijah told him to go again.
So once again the servant went down the **mountain**, through the **bushes**, over the **rocks**, down to the **beach** and there he **looked** out to **sea**.
Still there was nothing.

This went on all morning and by the time Elijah had told the servant to go and **look** for the seventh time he was getting rather tired.

But he went again, back down the **mountain**, through the **bushes**, over the **rocks**, down to the **beach** and there he **looked** out to **sea**.

And suddenly - he saw it, a tiny cloud coming over the horizon. (Say this quite fast) Quick as a flash he went back up the **beach**, over the **rocks**, through the **bushes** and up the **mountain**. And he told Elijah about the cloud.

"Quick," said Elijah. "Run!"

So quick as they could they went (Do this really fast) down the **mountain**, through the **bushes**, over the **rocks**, down to the **beach** and back home just as the **rain** came down.

Elijah on Mount Sinai

by Fiona Stewart-Darling

Angel - Flap wings   **Sleep** - Snore   **Frightened** - Look scared
Earthquake - Quiver   **Wind** - "Whoosh!"
Fire - "Crackle, crackle!" **Whisper** - Place finger to lips

Elijah was a prophet who lived many years ago. The queen at that time, who was called Jezebel, didn't like Elijah and wanted to kill him, so Elijah was very **frightened** and he ran away. He walked all day in the wilderness until he was tired and hot, and then he sat down in the cool shade of a tree. Elijah was very discouraged and fed up. He prayed to God: "It's too much, I can't go on, I just want to die!" And then he felt so tired that he fell **asleep**.

Suddenly an **angel** woke him up and told him to eat! There in front of him was a loaf of bread and a jar of water. So he ate and drank and went back to **sleep**. A second time the **angel** woke Elijah and told him to eat. The food gave Elijah the strength he needed to walk for forty days to a mountain called Mount Sinai, there he went into a cave to spend the night and **sleep**.

Suddenly God spoke to him: "Elijah, what are you doing here?"
Elijah, feeling very sorry for himself, answered, "Lord God Almighty, I have always obeyed you, but the Israelites have broken their promises to you and killed your prophets and now I am the only one left - and they want to kill me too! I'm **frightened**!"
So the Lord told Elijah to go and stand on top of the mountain. Then the Lord passed by and sent a furious **wind** that split the hills and shattered the rocks - but the Lord wasn't in the **wind**.
The **wind** stopped blowing, and then there was an **earthquake**... but the Lord was not in the **earthquake**. After the **earthquake** there was a **fire**... but the Lord was not in the **fire**. And after the **fire** - there was a soft **whisper** of a voice. When Elijah heard it he knew at once that it was God, so he covered his face with his cloak because he was afraid to look at God.

God spoke to him again. "Elijah, what are you doing here?"
Elijah, still feeling very sorry for himself, answered: "Lord God Almighty, I have always obeyed you, but the Israelites have broken their promises to you and killed your prophets and now I am the only one left, and they want to kill me too! I'm **frightened**!"

God reassured Elijah that he wasn't the only person left alive who trusted God - there were 7000 others! [Goodness knows how he missed them all!] God had come to find Elijah because he cared about him, and he didn't have to be **frightened** because God wanted to help him. So Elijah left the mountain and trusted God again, and did all things that God asked him to do.

Elisha Heals a Young Boy

This piece centres around parts of the body, and with a younger audience the responses may simply be to point to or touch the relevant bits as they are mentioned.

Hands - Wave hands   **Feet -** Stamp feet
Head - Clamp hands on side of head
Eyes - Blink twice   **Mouth** - Press hands to lips
Sneeze - Sneeze loudly   **Back** - Hold back and say "Ouch!"

Once a young boy was out working in the fields with his father. They were farmers, and it was very hard work. Hard on the **hands**, hard on the **feet**.
The boy sat down to rest his aching **back**, then suddenly he lifted his **hands** and clutched his **head**.
"I feel ill!" he cried. "My **head** hurts."
His father got a servant to carry him home, but he soon died there.
The boy's mother closed his **eyes** and laid him on a bed, then went looking for their friend, a man called Elisha, a man who believed in God and had a lot of faith.

Elisha came to their house and went to the room where the boy was lying. He looked at him, then slowly, very slowly, he touched the boy's **eyes** - with his own **eyes**. Then he touched the boy's **mouth** - with his own **mouth**. Finally he pressed his **hands** on the boy's **hands**.
Suddenly - the boy **sneezed**!
Then he **sneezed** again.
And **again**.
In fact - in all he **sneezed seven times**!
Then he opened his **eyes** and stood up on his **feet**.
Elisha called the boy's mother and showed her he was alive. She was so amazed, happy and thankful that she fell down with her **head** at Elisha's **feet**.

33
Isaiah and the King

Shh - Cover mouth   **Ditch** - Squelching mud
Problem - Scratch head   **Message** - Lick stamp   **Fight** - "Biff!"

In the days when King Hezekiah was in charge of Jerusalem, the Emperor of Assyria got together a huge army to **fight** and kill all the people in the cities nearby. Then he sent one of his men to Jerusalem with a **message** - to tell Hezekiah to give up and let him invade the city. The man stood in a **ditch** and Hezekiah sent three of his men to meet him. The man in the **ditch** said: "What makes you so confident? You can't **fight** us. Who's going to help you? Don't think that God will!"
"Shh!" said the three men, "don't say that, we don't want you scaring the rest of the city!"
But the man in the ditch wouldn't shut up, he made sure everyone could hear.
"Give up now!" he said, "or we'll **fight** and kill you all."
"Shh!" said the men, "everybody round here is listening!"
"Good!" said the man in the **ditch**, "I want everyone to know - don't listen to Hezekiah, God won't save you. If you trust us you'll be fine and happy, and you can have grapes and wine, and a good time. But if you trust God to save you - then you'll be eating mud - out of an old **ditch**! And you'll have a big **problem**!"
"Shh!" the men said again.
But the man laughed at them, climbed out of the **ditch** and walked off.
"Oh dear," said the three men, "I think we have a bit of a **problem**."

When the king heard the news he was very upset. He went to the temple to pray, and sent a **message** to Isaiah, who was a man of God. To the rest of the people in the city he simply said: "**Shh**!" And everybody kept quiet about the **problem**. Isaiah sent a **message** back saying:
"Don't panic - the Assyrians won't **fight** you - the Lord will sort out the **problem**."

But then the Emperor of Assyria sent Hezekiah another **message**:
"You've been told that God will save you - but don't listen to that. We're coming to **fight** you now, we smashed the other cities and we'll smash yours - so there!"
When Hezekiah read it the people asked him what to do - but he just said: "**Shh**! I'm trying to think!"
And he went off to the temple to pray for God's help again.

Then Isaiah sent a **message** from God to the Assyrians, telling them to back off, because God knew all about their **messages**, and all about the man in the **ditch**, and all about their **fights**, and they'd soon be running off home - because God would sort out the **problem**.

And that's exactly what happened. One night an angel from God crept into the Assyrian camp and when they all woke up the next morning - they were dead - in a **ditch**! And the Emperor had to run off home quickly - looking very embarrassed.

35
Ezekiel and the Dry Bones

Valley - Make sound of wind whistling through
Bones – Swing arm from elbow
Back to life - All look wide-eyed
Rattling – Rap knuckles on floor (or head)
Breathe - Breathe into hands   **Muscles** - Flex muscles
Pin drop - Let pin drop and say "Ding!"

God took Ezekiel and dropped him into a huge **valley** out in the desert. It was so quiet you could hear a **pin drop**. Ezekiel went for a walk through the **valley** and saw that the ground was covered with dry **bones**.
Just then God spoke to him, and he told Ezekiel to go through the **valley**, and speak to those **bones**, and to tell them that God was going to bring them back together with a loud **rattling noise** and then he was going to cover them with **muscles** and sinews and skin, and he was going to **breathe** into their bodies and bring them **back to life**.

So Ezekiel did what he was told and he commanded the **bones** to wake up. Suddenly Ezekiel heard a **rattling noise**, and he saw the **bones** join back together, then a wind blew through the **valley**, and it went over the **bones**. It gave them new sinews and skin and **muscles** - but they still didn't move, and it was still so quiet you could hear another **pin drop**. So Ezekiel commanded the wind to come and **breathe** new breath into the bodies, and like a film going backwards, they all came **back to life** and stood up. And God did the impossible, he made them live again!

And God said to Ezekiel, "My people often feel like those dry **bones**. They feel empty and dried up with no hope and no future. But I will **breathe** new hope into them and though they feel dead, I will bring them **back to life**."

Neb and the Men

Strange - Circle finger by temple; or shrug   **Neb** - Sit up straight!
Statue - Freeze in a pose   **Fire** - Roaring fire noises

Sometimes kings can be very proud - so proud that they think everyone should do everything they say. That was the case with **Nebuchadnezzar**. He had a very long name, and very **strange** ideas. For example - he built a **statue**. It couldn't walk, couldn't talk, couldn't do the homework, couldn't clean your room. It was very good at standing still though, and **Nebuchadnezzar** thought everybody should get on their knees and bow to it. Not only that - but he decided that everyone should do it whenever he played some music -   a bit like musical chairs. Or musical **statues**! And he thought that this was such a good idea that he threatened that if anyone refused they would be thrown into a huge **fire** and burnt. Kings can be very **strange**!

Now **Neb**, as we'll call him - but don't tell him, he may not like it - **Neb** had lots of men that worked for him, and three of them were brilliant at their jobs. They were very clever, so clever that they would not bow to any **statue**. That didn't seem a good idea to them. They only bowed to God. So when the music started - and everybody else hit the deck, these three carried on working as brilliantly as ever.

So **Neb** had what he thought was another good idea - he decided to throw his three best men into a large **fire**. He thought that might help them. **Strange**! So he very bravely ordered 50 of his strongest men to tie the three of them up and throw them into the **fire**.
And that was when he had yet another good idea - he made the **fire** so hot that when his best soldiers went near it - they all got killed as well! Good ol' **Neb**!

Then he had a shock, because he looked into the **fire** and he could see four people walking inside it, not three, and they didn't seem to be having much trouble in there, not even the odd   blister. He counted again and could still see four people, not three - and one of them looked like an angel!

So he had them pulled out of the **fire** and suddenly there was only three - but they were completely unharmed, didn't even smell of smoke.

So **Neb** said: "Right, nobody is allowed to hurt these three men. They wouldn't bow down to the **statue**, because they would only worship God. I think they're brilliant!"

Strange! This was a bit of a U-turn for **Neb** of course. Then he had one last good idea. If anyone even thought anything bad about these three he would have them killed - ripped apart - slaughtered - smashed - bopped on the head. In other words - more of his own good men down the drain! Good ol' **Neb** - kings do have some rather **strange** ideas!

Jonah and the Whale

Hero - Say "Huh" and adopt macho stance   **Star** - "Thank you, fans!"
Boat - Start up motor-boat   **Holiday** - Put on shades
Overboard - "Aggghhhhh!!!"   **Threw him up** - "Blughhh!"
Swallowed - "Ulp!"   **Smell** - "Phawww!"

Jonah was a guy who didn't want to.
He didn't want to be a big **hero**. He didn't want to be a big **star**. He just wanted a nice easy life. With no worries.
So - one day, when he heard a voice telling him to get on a **boat** and go and tell some people who lived on a big island about God, he decided the best thing to do was to go on **holiday**.
He had obviously working too hard.
After all - he didn't want to be a big **hero**. And do anything dangerous.
And he didn't want to be a big **star**.
He just wanted to be on **holiday**.

So he got on a **boat** and went in the opposite direction. And he was very happy.
However, that's when he made his big mistake - he forgot to take his money, to pay for the **boat** ride and when the ticket man came round Jonah had a brilliant idea - he tried to hide in the ash tray. But of course, he couldn't get in.
And as the ticket man gently threw him **overboard**, he landed in the sea, and guess what - a massive fish came and **swallowed** him!

Luckily for Jonah it wasn't a shark - so it didn't chew him - he was **swallowed** whole. It was quite amazing really! But Jonah didn't think about that - after all he didn't want to be a **hero**, and he didn't want to be a **star** - right then he just wanted to be somewhere else. Anywhere else. And so the fish agreed, because Jonah was giving him a bad stomach ache. So it carefully **threw him up** on a rather nice beach - on the very island that God wanted Jonah to visit. All the people could **smell** Jonah a mile off, so they all came to see what the **smell** was all about.

And that's when Jonah discovered that he didn't have to be a big **hero**, or a big **star**. He just had to be himself, and do what God wanted him to do.

And while they hosed him down on the beach he told them how he'd come such a long way and been **swallowed** by a massive fish, which had **thrown him up** on the beach just so that he could tell them all how much God cared about them.

The Jonah Factor

Hero - Say "Huh" and adopt macho stance
Star - "Thank you, fans! Thank you!"
Bible   - Clap hands once, and open them, book-like
Train   - Pinch nose, say "Welcome to British Rail"
Witness - Hold up right hand, say "YEP!" or "YO!"

You may recognise huge similarities between this and the previous piece! This version came first, written with teenagers in mind, but I then adapted it for younger children, and created the other version which follows the Biblical account a little more closely.

Jonah was a guy who didn't want to.
He didn't want to be a **hero**. He didn't want to be a **star**. He didn't want to be anyone. He just wanted an easy life.
So - one day, when he read in his **Bible** that maybe God wanted him to be a **witness** to his next door neighbour, he decided the best thing to do was take a holiday.
He was obviously working too hard.
After all - he didn't want to be a **hero**.
And he didn't want to be a **star**.
He wanted to be a holiday maker.

So he got on a **train**. And he was very happy.
So happy that he forgot to take his **Bible**   - just in case God tried to talk to him again. After all - there are no **Bibles** on trains!
However, that's when he made his big mistake - he forgot to take his **train** fare as well, and when the inspector came round Jonah had a brilliant idea - he tried to hide in the ash tray. But of course, he couldn't get in - the ash tray was already full - with three fag ends and a good news **Bible**...
[Strangely enough.]
And as the inspector gently threw him out of the window, he landed on a passing dustcart, amongst the broken bottles, dirty nappies and an unusually large amount of good news **Bibles**!

However, Jonah didn't want to be a **hero**, and he didn't want to be a **star** - right then he just wanted to be somewhere else. Anywhere else. And so the dustcart willingly obliged, and it carefully tipped him out in a rather large pile of **Bibles** right onto the doorstep of his next door neighbour - who happily came to the door to discover what the smell was all about. Just then, everybody in the street came to the door to discover what the smell was all about. And that's when Jonah discovered that at that moment he didn't have to be a **hero**, or a **star**. He just had to be a **witness**.

And while they hosed him down in the driveway he told them how he'd come such a long way just to be with them all. And they were so impressed they all took a **Bible**.

So if you don't want to be a **hero**, and you don't want to be a **star**, then that's a very good sign - you could be a **witness**.

Mary and the Angel

Kitchen - Kitchen sounds   **Bread** - Spread butter on hand
White - Look shocked   **Excited** - Rub hands together
Wedding - Wedding bells

Mary was very **excited**, because very soon she was going to get married. One day, while she was in the **kitchen** making some **bread** and thinking about the **wedding**, she suddenly saw a bright light appear outside in the hall. She ran out of the **kitchen**, still carrying the bread and thinking about the **wedding**, and almost bumped into a very tall man, wearing dazzling **white** clothes, with a very bright face.

Mary wasn't sure whether to be frightened or **excited** at meeting this person - he certainly was very **white**.
"Don't be afraid!" said the man in **white**, "I've got good news for you!"
Mary did start feeling afraid and she went very **white**.
"God wants to help you, Mary," the man went on, "you are going to have a baby - and God wants you to call him Jesus. He will be the Son of God - and he will be a King who will be in charge forever."

The man seemed very **excited** about this - but Mary wasn't so sure. What about her **wedding**? She wasn't even married yet.
"This child will be a miracle baby," said the man, "he will be God's baby - different to any other person."
Mary was so amazed that she dropped the **bread** on the floor, and ran back into the **kitchen**. But the man in **white** didn't seem to mind, he said goodbye and when Mary looked again he had gone.

For a long time she sat in the **kitchen**, with the **bread** in her hands, thinking about the man in **white**, and about her **wedding**, and about God's baby. And the more she thought - the more she felt very **excited**.

The Inn

Dark and stormy - Storm noises   **Teeth** - Mime cleaning teeth
Door - "Creak"   **Hair** - "Doiing!"   **Knock** - Knock once
Tired - Yawn   **Shed** - "Ugh!"

It was a **dark and stormy** night, and the manager of the Bethlehem Inn was very **tired**. The hotel was full and he'd had a long hard day, and all he wanted was a nice rest. So he shut the hotel **door** and climbed the stairs to his luxury bedroom. Just as he got into bed he remembered that he hadn't cleaned his **teeth**, so he got out, cleaned his **teeth** and staggered back.

Outside it was still a **dark and stormy** night - and suddenly there was a sharp **knock** on the **door**. The manager sat up and listened. There it was again - one sharp knock. The manager wasn't sure who it might be and he was very **tired**, but he got out again, re-cleaned his **teeth**, and went down the stairs. As he reached for the **door** there was another **knock**. The manager's **hair** stood on end, but he plucked up his courage and opened the **door**. Outside it was **dark and stormy** - but there was no one there. So he quickly shut the **door**, and ran up stairs to bed. Suddenly there was another **knock**. The manager's **hair** stood up again. And so did he. He was so frightened that he cleaned his **teeth** again, and went to the **door**. There was no one there - but outside it was very **dark and stormy**. He stepped outside to look round, and suddenly felt a hand touch his shoulder. "Aah!" he jumped and turned round. There was a man - looking very white. He had a woman with him - and she looked **tired** and frightened.

The man's name was Joseph - and he asked if they could have a room for the night. The manager told them to go away, and he shut the **door**. Half an hour later he was still awake - although he was **tired**, he couldn't sleep. Suddenly - there was another **knock** on the door. This time his **hair** didn't stand on end, but he jumped up and ran down the stairs. It was Joseph again. Every hotel was full - and could they please stay in the dirty old **shed** at the back of the hotel? The night was still very **dark and stormy**, so the manager gave in and very kindly let them sleep in the old **shed** out at the back.

An hour later there was yet another **knock** on the **door**. The manager couldn't believe it. This time it was a group of excited shepherds. Could they see the baby please? The manager was about to strangle them all when they heard a baby's cry - coming from the old **shed** at the back. They all rushed outside - through the **dark and stormy** night - and there they saw the baby, wrapped up in an old sheet where he had just been born in that dirty old **shed**. The mother looked very **tired**. Joseph looked amazed. The shepherds all knelt down - and the manager wondered just what on earth was going on.

The Nativity

Animals - Animal sounds
Baby - Cradle baby in arms
Angel - Look amazed
Star - Look through telescope
Bethlehem - Hand over eyes, look round

These response stories might be useful in a class or workshop as an easy way to get the group into doing some drama. Just teach them the responses and then tell the story. They may like to do it as one large group, or you could divide them into small groups. You might also tell them the key words, but then ask them to think up an appropriate noise and action. You could give each group one word to respond to.

Mary and Joseph had travelled all night. It was a long journey, and Mary was very uncomfortable because she was about to have a **baby**. When they got to **Bethlehem**, which was the place they were heading for, they tried to find somewhere to stay the night - but everywhere was full. So Mary had her **baby** in a stable, where **animals** lived, and they wrapped the baby in pieces of cloth to keep him warm and then they laid him down in the trough that the **animals** ate from. They called the **baby** Jesus, and he was the Son of God.

That same night, while Mary had her **baby**, there were some shepherds nearby in a field and they were looking after their sheep. An **angel** appeared to them in the sky, looking very bright, and they were all afraid. But the **angel** told them not to be frightened, and told them about Mary's **baby**. Then a huge crowd of **angels** appeared in the sky, singing beautiful songs and praising God.

When the **angels** went back to heaven the shepherds decided to go and visit the **baby**, so they went to **Bethlehem**, looked high and low, and found Mary and Joseph.

They knew that this was the **baby** Jesus, because the **angel** had told them that he would be wrapped up in pieces of cloth and lying in an **animal** trough. They told Mary and Joseph about the **angels** and everyone was amazed.

Then the shepherds went back to their field talking, laughing and singing praises to God, just like the **angels** had been doing.

Not long after this some men who studied the **stars** came looking for Jesus from another country, because they had seen a special **star** in the sky which showed them that this **baby** was a king. First they went to King Herod in a place called Jerusalem, but he didn't know anything about it. He hadn't seen the **star** or heard any **angels**. So he asked some of his advisors and they told him to look in **Bethlehem**. So the men set off again and they saw the **star** they had been following, and it made them very happy.

The **star** stopped over a house and when they went in they found Mary and Joseph there with Jesus, so they quickly took out some presents, gave them to him and then worshipped him. Then they got up and left, and didn't go back to King Herod because an **angel** told them not to, instead they went back home to their own country.

The Two Houses

Divide the audience into two halves.
One half stand and cheer on the word "**Clever**";
the other half stand and cheer on the word "**Other**".
House/Houses - All make house shape with hands and say "ping!"
Foundations - All bend down and knock on the floor

Two men decided to build their own **houses**. One of the men was very, very, very **clever** - the **other** man wasn't.
The **clever** one had 27 G.C.S.E.'s.   The **other** one didn't.
The **clever** one had loads of money. The **other** one didn't.
So, when they decided to build their **houses** the **clever** one already knew lots about how to do it, and he went straight off to his building site and started work.

But the **other** one, well, he didn't know a lot about building **houses**, so he went off - and found someone else who did.
They both worked hard for a long time.
Suddenly - both men finished their **houses** and the weather began to change. Before long a massive storm was battering both **houses**.

Now, both **houses** were made of bricks and good strong steel; both had weatherproof paint and lots of drain pipes.
But only one fell down.
The **clever** man's **house**... didn't survive, it collapsed - because he built his **house** on a swamp by mistake, and he didn't check the **foundations**.
The **other** man's **house** stayed up - because he may not have been **clever** - but he did ask for help. So to be **clever** doesn't always mean you are wise.

To be wise means that you don't always rely on yourself - you get help... and you check your **foundations**!

The Good Samaritan

Hurt - Hold leg and say: "Ow!"   **Headache** - "Throb, throb, throb!"
Meeting - Make sounds of rowdy politicians   **Tripped** - "Oops!"
Priest - Big smile   **Help** - Raise hand enthusiastically to volunteer

This story ends by throwing a question at the audience. It also finishes with the man not being rescued by the Good Samaritan! This is designed to make the audience think and to help us realise that the story is really about ourselves. So you may like to brainstorm afterwards about opportunities we often miss, and why it can be quite frightening, and sometimes dangerous, to reach out and help people.

Once there was a man who was on a journey, walking from a place called Jerusalem, to a place called Jericho. It was a long way, and the man soon got tired so he sat down to have a rest. Suddenly he was surrounded by a gang of men who grabbed him and asked him for his money. When he tried to run away, they **tripped** him up, knocked him over and beat him up. When he woke up, they'd all gone, and so had his money. He tried to stand up, but his legs really **hurt** and he had a bad **headache**, so he lay down again.

Just then a **priest** went past in a great hurry, he looked at the man but the sight of blood made him feel ill, so although the **priest** wanted to **help** - he didn't and quickly hurried on. Then a woman went past so quickly she almost **tripped** over the man who was **hurt**. She was a politician but she didn't stop because she had a very important **meeting** to attend. It was a **meeting** about homeless people. So the man still lay there on the ground. His legs still **hurt** and his **headache** just got worse and worse. Three days later he died.

There used to be a story about a man who was **helped** by the Good Samaritan who stopped and took him to a hospital - but he didn't go by at all during those three days, so he couldn't **help** the man. You and I both went past the man too, I didn't notice him myself... how about you?

The Good Tramp

There are fifteen responses accompanying this story, you may like to choose just a few. Originally it was written as part of a school show, and some of the audience were invited out to present the piece, which is the reason for the number of responses, it's part way between a sketch and a response story.

Posh businessman - "Oh, I say"   **Bus Stop** - "Ding! Ding!"
Dirty - "Phaw!"   **Teacher** - Sit very still
Hospital - Siren noise   **Sorry** - "Ahhhh!"
Scared - Hold stomachs   **Tramp** - Big sniff, wipe nose on hand
Ground - Fall down   **Big House** - "Wow!" Look up
Money - "Chink"   **Wallet** - Hand on chest
Watch - Hand on wrist   **Vicar** - Shake hands /Give five say "Yo!"
Football supporters - Shout for different football teams (different groups)

I mentioned in the introduction (all those pages ago!) that it is a good tool to involve the audience in competition. This story relies heavily on this, as the audience should be divided into halves or quarters then each side allocated with a favourite football team to support. It is best to ask one person in each group to nominate a favourite team for their group to shout for. This may be a local side or one of the popular division teams. N.B. You won't please all the people all the time so you may have to be firm about the whole group shouting for the same team!

Once, there was a **bus stop**. And there were three people waiting at this **bus stop**. First, there was a **posh businessman**; he had a very **big house**, and lots of **money**.
Then there was the local **vicar**. He had quite a **big house**, and quite a lot of **money**, but not as much as the **posh businessman**. The third person there was called Dougal.
Now Dougal was a very **smelly tramp** because he didn't have a **big house**, or very much **money**, and he lived in a cardboard box. And he didn't have any friends - because he was such a **smelly tramp**.

Well, just then, a gang of **football supporters** went running past. And these **football supporters** made a lot of noise. They didn't notice the **posh businessman**, the **vicar** or the **tramp** - but they did see the school **teacher** coming the other way. And as they got to the **bus stop**, the **football supporters** grabbed him and threw him to the **ground**. Then they stole his **wallet**, his **watch**, and all his **money**. Then they ran off, leaving him lying on the **ground**.

Just then, the **bus** arrived. The **posh businessman** looked at the **teacher**, who was lying very still on the **ground**, then he quickly jumped on the **bus** - because he was **scared** of the sight of blood.
The **vicar** - well, he looked at the **teacher**, lying there on the **ground**, then he saw the **posh businessman** jump on the **bus**, and he decided to do the same, because he was **scared** of   **football supporters**.

Now, Dougal, the **smelly tramp**, when he saw the **teacher**, he felt **sorry** for him. So he went over to the **teacher**, and helped him up. Then he gave him 50p which was all the **money** he'd got from begging. And even though Dougal was very **smelly**, the **teacher** didn't mind, because Dougal took him to a **hospital** and made sure that he was okay. Dougal the **tramp** acted like a very good friend.

51
The Friend at Midnight

Called out - "Go away!"   **Window** - Open creaking window
Toe - "Ow!"   **Bed** - Snuggle against hands
Water - "Splash!"   **Sugar** - "Mmm!"

I had just gone to **bed** the other night when what should happen? I heard this knock on the door! There I am - tucked up safely in **bed**, and someone's knocking on my door. I pretended I was still asleep but they kept on knocking! It was terrible, so I crept over to the **window**, opened it up and **called out**: "*Go away!*" Then I ran back to **bed**, and stubbed my **toe** on the floor. Two minutes later, there it was again - another knock. So this time I got a glass of **water**, went to the **window** and tipped it over the person at my door, then I **called out:**   But two minutes later they were back.

So this time I got a whole bucket of **water**, went to the **window** and tipped it all over them, then I **called out:**   But two minutes later they were back again.
So I ran down the stairs, stubbing my **toe** as I went, and I opened the door and **called out:**
But they didn't. It was my next door neighbour - covered in **water**!
"What do you want?" I said, "I was in **bed**."
"Can I borrow a cup of **sugar**?"
"What? I said, "you got me out of **bed** for that?"
"No," he said, "I want three loaves of bread as well! Oh - and a towel too!"
Well, I was so angry I just shut the door and went back to **bed**, stubbing my **toe** on the way.

But he wouldn't go away! He just kept knocking. So I ignored it. I shut the **window** and hid under my **bed**. So he went and got a trumpet and began playing "*God save the Queen*" outside. So I ran all the way back down and threw open the door.
"Can I have a cup of **sugar** and three loaves of bread?" he said.
"Yes!" I said, "but only if you go away!"

He didn't have a cup so I had to lend him that as well. And a bag for the bread, and some Flora, and some tea and milk to go with the **sugar**, and some hot **water**, and some chocolate biscuits, and a bread knife, and a cupboard to put it all in, and finally my own car so that he could get it all home. Then for the last time I **called out:**

And he did. For half an hour. Then he ran out of ice-cream... and coffee... and Weetabix... and money... and clothes... and Lego... and a TV licence... We've swopped houses now. It's easier that way.

And it just goes to show - persistence does work!

The Lost Sheep

Farmer - "Ooh arr!"   **Droppings** - "Squelch squelch!"
Sheep - "Baa!"   **Run away** - Jog on the spot
3 o'clock - "Bong, bong, bong!"   **Barbed wire** - "OUCH!"
Searched/Searching - Whistle for sheep

This story contains the key word *Droppings*! It is quite useful with children to throw in slightly messy or 'naughty' images, as they do enjoy this!

There was once a **farmer** with rather a lot of **sheep**. In fact he had more **sheep** than any other **farmer** nearby. He was the best **sheep farmer** for miles.

But one day one of his **sheep** decided to **run away**. "I think I'll **run away**!" he said. And so he did - he **ran away** for miles looking for a life with better fields, greener grass and no mint sauce. Now when the **farmer** came round that night all that he found was a trail of **droppings** in the street and he guessed what had happened.

So he headed down the town, following the **droppings** and checking all the restaurants to see if any of them were serving up lamb stew.
He **searched** everywhere - he **searched** high an' low - hour after hour - he didn't eat - he didn't sleep - he just kept on **searching**. Even when it was almost **3 o'clock** in the morning - he didn't give up but kept on looking for the **sheep** as if it was the only thing he owned.

Then at last - at dead on **3 o'clock** - he heard a faint bleating sound from behind a hedge. He looked over and sure enough - there was the **sheep**! He had **run away** into the field and was caught in some **barbed wire**.
His nose was all bashed and his little feet were all bruised. (*Aaahh...*)

But the **farmer** took one look at him, gently pulled him out of the **barbed wire** and carried him all the way back to the farm. When he got home the whole farm was overjoyed, because the **sheep** which had **run away** had been found again and brought home safely.

The Prodigal Son

Money - Count out notes   **X-Box** - Computer noises
Brilliant - Say "Yes!" and punch the air
Food - Chewing sounds   **Sons** - Flex muscles   **Work** - Wipe brow
Party - Hand jive/Dance   **Jeans** - "How much!!"
Milkshakes - Make sucking sound

This parable has been altered slightly, it's the lazy one who stays with his father and the hardworking son who runs away. This is to make the audience think again about the story. When Jesus told his parables they often surprised people, so sometimes it's worth turning stories on their head to make the people who already know them, think again. You might like to try this with other parables.

Once there was a man who had two **sons**. They were called Simon and Adrian. Simon was hard **working** and enthusiastic but his brother, Adrian, was just the opposite. He stayed in bed every day until 11 o'clock, then he would get up and play with his **X-Box**, before going out to McDonalds and eating four Big Macs and three large **milkshakes**.

Then one day one of the **sons** decided he'd had enough and wanted to leave home, so he got hold of a gun and went to his father and ordered him to give him all the **money** in the house. His father was very shocked and sad, but he gave him all the **money** and the **son** ran off.

He went to the big city and as soon as he arrived he went to the shops, took out his **money** and bought five new pairs of **jeans** and 16 pairs of trainers; then he got his hair cut, bought a new **X-Box** and then went to the pub and bought drinks for everybody there - until they were all really drunk. Everyone thought he was **brilliant**, and they became his friends. Then he fell asleep in a chair. When he woke up he found that his new friends had stolen all his **money**, his **jeans**, his trainers, and his **X-Box**. He was broke and had no **food**.

He tried to get a job, but because he had no home address, no one would let him **work**. So he started sleeping in a cardboard box on the streets and begging for **food** from the people who went past. Then one day he he remembered that his father used to pay people to clean out the drains of their house, so he decided to go home and see if he could **work** for his dad.

It took him three days to walk there; he had no **food**, no **money**, and his shoes fell apart on the way. As he got near the house he heard his father scream and shout, and he thought his father was going to kill him. But he was too tired to run away, and the next thing he knew the old man had grabbed him and given him a really big hug - he was so happy to see his **son** again. And before he could ask if he could clean the gutters, they pulled him inside the house, gave him loads of **food** and a new pair of **jeans** and called all the neighbours round for a **party**!

Now... Which son was it?
Not Adrian - he was still down at McDonalds drinking his **milkshake**. It was Simon, the hard **working** one, who had left home. When Simon came back and Adrian heard about the **party** he was very angry. "It's not fair! Simon's lost all your **money** and you never give me a **party**!" he said. "Well, you're always out at McDonalds," his father said, "but we had to celebrate now - because I thought Simon was dead - but he's alive! And that's **brilliant**!"

The Prodigal Son [2]

Anonymous; adapted

Father - Put hand on stiff back   **Money** - Throw notes in the air
Servant - Stand and bow   **Wept** - Sniff and wipe eyes   **Party** -
Shout "Cheers!" and raise glasses   **Stew** - "Slurp!"

There once was a **father** who had two sons,
They lived on a farm - had lots of fun;
The younger one came to his **father** and said:
"Give me some **money** - I'm off to the Med!"

Well, his **father** cried and he **wept** all day,
But in the end he said: "Okay".
So off the son went, **money** in hand,
He travelled all the way to a far-off land.

He raved all night and he **partied** all day -
Riotous living - whey hey hey!
Spent all his time messing around
And wasting his **money** like a foolish clown.

Then one day his **money** ran out.
So did the food, because of a drought.
His friends all left him feeding swine -
And that's when he knew things weren't too fine.

He thought of home in days gone by,
Where they had baked beans and apple pie.
His **father** had **servants** who never got the sack -
So he came to his senses and said, "I'll go back!"

He ran right back to his **father's** land,
Knelt at his feet and kissed his hand;
He said he was sorry for being a berk! Said:
"Do you need a **servant** - 'cause I need the work!"

His **father** cried and **wept** for joy.
He shouted out: "Look, here's my boy!
Put rings on his fingers and shoes on his feet
And lets have a **party** with loads to eat."

You may like to finish the story here. The following two verses are additions to the actual story. Sometimes it's better though to leave it to the audience to think about the meaning and application without spoonfeeding it to them...

So what's the point of this little poem?
Who's the son who ran away from ho-em (!);
Who left his **father** and got in a **stew**?
Have you ever thought that it might be you?

Well, you never know - it might be you.
One day you may land in the **stew**!
All alone with nothing to do...
Well, remember this story 'cause it's just for you.

Jesus and the Little Girl

Ill - Hold stomach in pain   **Laughed/Laughing** - All laugh
House - "Ding dong"   **Eyes** - Blink twice, eyes wide

Once, when Jesus was walking along talking and **laughing** with his disciples, a man came up to him and begged him to come to his **house** and help his little girl. She was very **ill** and no-one could help her - not even the doctors. So Jesus went with the man, but as they got nearer to his **house** the man was told that his little girl was dead, and it was no use bringing Jesus to see her. Jesus told the man not to worry - he said: "Don't worry, she will be alright."

This seemed a strange thing to say, but they carried on into the **house**. Inside everyone was crying, but Jesus said to them all, "Don't cry, she's not dead, she is only asleep."
Some of them **laughed** at this, because they knew that she had been **ill** and they had even seen her die. Jesus went into her bedroom and saw the little girl lying very still on the bed. Her **eyes** were closed and she wasn't breathing at all but Jesus took her hand and said to her, "Get up!"

For a second nothing happened, then suddenly she moved, her **eyes** flicked open, and she sat up in bed, very much alive. She smiled at Jesus and Jesus asked her parents to go and get her some food. Soon she was up and about, talking and **laughing** again. They were all amazed at this, it was no ordinary day - but then Jesus was no ordinary person.

The Widow's Mite

by Kevin Huggett

Watched - Put your hands to your eyes   **Crowd** - "Bustle, bustle!"
Rich people - Push thumbs under lapels   **Money** - "Chink, chink!"
Widow - "Shuffle, shuffle" [Quietly]   **Coin** - Drop coin, "Plink!"

One day, after walking for a long time with his friends the disciples, Jesus was very tired and he found a place to sit down in the temple in Jerusalem. As he rested Jesus **watched** the **crowd** of people coming in and out. He often sat and **watched** people, this time he was sitting next to the place where people brought their offerings of **money** to God. They put their **money** into a big wooden box.

As Jesus **watched** the **crowd** he saw that in the **crowd** were a lot of very **rich people**, who walked proudly and confidently into the temple with their **money** bags chinking loudly. These **rich people** put lots and lots of **money** into the box. "God must be pleased with them," thought Jesus as he **watched**.

After Jesus had **watched** for a while a poor, poor **widow** appeared at the edge of the **crowd**.
"She can't have any **money** at all," thought Jesus, "and she looks so sad and tired." The **widow** shuffled quietly forward to the big wooden box and pulled something out of her ragged clothes. All the **rich people** tried to ignore her so they looked away and talked to each other, but Jesus watched very carefully.
The **widow** brought out one little copper **coin** and dropped it into the box. Then she pulled out a second **coin** and put that one in too. The **coins** were worth almost nothing at all, but Jesus knew they were all that the **widow** had.

Jesus called the disciples together and said, "Did you notice the **crowd** putting their **money** in the box?" And he told them about the **widow** and said, "The **rich people** gave a little bit out of the many good things they have, but the **widow**, who had almost nothing, put in all she had to live on because she loves God so much."

Do Not Worry

Worry - Say "Ahh!" and look scared   **Mumps** - Blow out cheeks
Fleas - Scratch   **Love** - Make kissing sound   **Earthquake** - Shudder
Birthday - Blow out candles   **Christmas** - Pull cracker, say "Bang!"

A good way to introduce a response story is to pick an amusing key word, demonstrate the funny response and then ask everyone if they can do this response. With this story I often start by looking very scared and I then ask everyone if they can do that same expression. This usually gets a laugh and I then I explain why I would like them to try this.

One day Jesus gathered all the people around him and he began to talk to them.
He said:
"You could **worry** about tomorrow.
There might be an **earthquake**;
or an epidemic of **fleas**;
or **both**.

You might fall in **love**;
or catch **mumps**;
or fall in **love** and catch **mumps**.
It may be your **birthday**,
or **Christmas**,
or **both**!
But don't **worry**.

Instead, keep looking to God for help.
After all, do the flowers **worry**?
Do the birds **worry**?
Does the grass **worry**?
And yet God looks after them.

So don't **worry** about tomorrow. It may be **Christmas**, and you might fall in **love** - but God knows about it, and He'll be there.

The Sower

Lawn - Lean back in seat as if in a deck chair,
with your hands behind your head
Seeds - Mime scattering a handful of seed
Blackbirds - Make bird sounds   **Gobbled** - Make chewing noises
Rocks/Rockery - "Ouch!" **Manure** - Sniff and say "Ugh!"
Bushes - Splay out fingers like spiky branches

Once there was a woman who moved into a brand new house. She decided to grow a nice green **lawn** in her back garden so she went out and scattered lots of grass **seed** everywhere.

Some of the **seed** fell on the concrete footpath and at lunch time some huge **blackbirds** flew down and **gobbled** it all up.
Some of the seed fell on the **rockery** at the far end of the garden, where there was a lot of **rocks** but not much soil, and when it started to **rain** in the afternoon the grass **seeds** got washed away because they had nowhere to put down their roots.

Some of the grass **seed** fell in the **bushes**, and it got snagged up in the prickly branches of the **bushes** and couldn't grow properly.
But some of the **seed** fell on the nice new soil, which had lots of ripe **manure** spread on it, and before too long the grass had sprouted and grown up into a lovely new bright green **lawn**.

The Two Sons

When any **number** is mentioned hold up appropriate amount of fingers.
This includes words that *sound* like numbers e.g. **to**, **for** and **ate**.

This style of response can be applied to many stories which involve numbers. It is educational because of the counting involved, but also a lot of fun when people get their fingers and thumbs tied up in knots! How fast you deliver the story is up to you, but it might be an idea to start slow then gradually speed up and see what happens!

One man had **two** sons and **one** day this man asked   **one** of the sons **to** do a job **for** him. He asked him **to** clean the family car, a Nissan   **four** by **four**. That **one** son agreed, but then did **nothing** and went off instead to watch his football team lose **six** - **three**. **Five** hours later when the father **ate** his tea he discovered that the job had not been done.

So he went **to** the other son, the younger **one**, and asked him **to** do the job **for** him. But the son gave **three** reasons why he wouldn't do it and went off and **ate** his tea. **Ten** minutes later at **twenty** past **seven** the man went **to** clean the **four** by **four** himself, and what should he find but **one** of the sons with **sixteen** friends - all cleaning the family car. Which left the man **nothing** to do.

Now - **three** questions - which son was it? Why did he do it? And where did he find **sixteen** friends?
One - it was the younger son.
Two - he did it because he changed his mind.
Three - he was a very popular guy! Not because of the things he said - but because of the things he did - that's what mattered.

For it wasn't the **first** son who did the right thing - he did **nothing** - but it was the younger **one** - he got it right.

The Farm

Divide the audience into five different sections. Each section represents the following five characters/people/things and should make their appropriate response on hearing their key word.

Section One:	**The Farmer** -	Stand up and rub hands, contented
Section Two:	**The Servant** -	Stand and bow/grovel
Section Three:	**The Son** -	Say: "Yo!"
Section Four:	**The Workers** -	Evil laugh "Hee hee hee!"
Section Five:	**The Farm** -	Various farm noises

In this story the audience is divided into groups or sections, and so each section needs only to remember one response. This is something you can do with any of the stories, simply divide the group or congregation into clearly defined smaller groups and then allocate a response to each group. You might like to ask them to stand up whenever they make their given response, and if the story is told quite fast then this becomes quite amusing.

This is the story of a **farm**, and a **farmer** who had a **servant** and a **son**. One day he decided to get some help on his **farm**, so he hired some **workers**. He showed them what to do, then left them to run the **farm**.

A few days later the **farmer** sent his **servant** to see how the **workers** were doing, but when they saw him coming the **workers** placed a bucket of pig swill over the top of the **farm**house door, and when the **servant** came in it fell on his head. The **servant** wasn't too happy about this and he went back to the **farmer** to complain. The **farmer** sent him back again to find out what the **workers** were up to, so this time the **workers** threw rotten tomatoes at him and dropped a cowpat onto his head.

When he got back the **farmer** told him to go again but the **servant** had had enough for one day, so the **son** cheerfully offered to go and see the **workers**. The **farmer** decided that they wouldn't hurt his **son**, so he let him visit the **farm**.

When they saw the **son** coming the **workers** decided to beat him up, and then take over the **farm** completely. They jumped on the **son** and attacked him.

A few minutes later the **farmer** himself arrived and he saw his **son** on the floor, lying very still. He was dead - they had killed him. So the **farmer** brought a large gang of his **servants** to the **farm**, and they threw the **workers** out so that they could never come back to the **farm** again.

The Big Party

Party - Party sounds   **Food** - Lick lips
Hats - Mime pulling on hat
Records - Dance movements   **Football** - Call out favourite team
Trivial Pursuit - Say: "Ummm...?" as if trying to think of an answer

Some stories work well on the street. If the responses make sense for unchurched people, and if the story is appropriate for telling outside, then why not try one in an open-air event? You might like to adjust the responses to make them bigger and more like pantomime. The more zany the story, the better! And of course the typical "Oh yes you can - oh no you can't!" responses work very well.

There was a rich man who decided to have a very big **party**. He ordered loads of **food**, lots of funny **hats** and all the latest *Coldplay* (or appropriate pop group) **records**. Then he sent out a big pile of invitations - telling all his rich relatives and friends about the **party**.

But when his relatives heard about the **party** they couldn't be bothered to go - instead they stayed in to watch the **football** on TV. When his friends heard about it they were jealous of all the man's **food**, **party** hats and *Oasis* **records**; so they didn't go either, they stayed in and played *Trivial Pursuit* instead.
When the man opened the doors and no-one came he was very upset.
Then he had an idea.

There were lots of poor people and homeless people living near his house, so he went out and asked them to come to his **party**.
So they did come and they had a wonderful time. They ate all the **food**, played the **records** and put on the funny **hats**.

And all the rich man's relatives and friends missed out completely on the good time because they were playing *Trivial Pursuit* and watching the **football** - but all the poor people came, and they soon became the rich man's friends.

The Easter Story - Part One - Friday

Soldiers - Salute and say "Sir!"   **Frightened/ening** - Look scared
Friends - Shake hands with someone near   **People** - Jeer and shout
Nails - Press thumb in palm of other hand   **Cross** - Hit palm with fist

This is a very serious story, so I have written it in such a way that the responses are serious, not humorous. This requires careful storytelling, building the atmosphere and suspense through the manner of the delivery by the narrator.

It was a very strange and **frightening** time. Jesus and his **friends** met together on that Thursday evening in a room upstairs where they had a meal together. Jesus gave them bread and wine and told them to always remember him whenever they did this in the future. His **friends** didn't really understand this, but they agreed to do it. Then Jesus washed their feet, and then led them out to the garden of Gethsemane. His **friends** fell asleep there - but not Jesus, he stayed awake praying and talking to God. He seemed quite upset. Suddenly a large crowd of **people**, some of them **soldiers**, attacked the group and dragged Jesus away. The **friends** all ran off - except for Peter and John, who followed at a safe distance.

The next part was very confusing and **frightening**, but Jesus was taken from one place to another to be accused and knocked about by the **people** who had arrested him. Peter, while trying to find out what was going on, was spotted as being one of Jesus' **friends**, but he lied about it and managed to escape. Then a man called Pontius Pilate took Jesus outside in front of all the **people** and asked them what he should do. Everyone shouted out "*Crucify him!*" - though lots of them didn't really know what they were saying. Pontius Pilate didn't want to do it but he was **frightened** and agreed to the demands of the **people**.

So the **soldiers** gave Jesus a massive, wooden **cross** to carry and made him carry it through the crowds of jeering **people** up to a hill called Calvary. He fell down on the way, it was so heavy, but someone helped him and eventually they got to the top.

Then they made Jesus lie down while they hammered large **nails** through his hands and feet and into the **cross**. Then they lifted up the **cross** and dropped it into a hole in the ground so that Jesus was hanging there by the **nails**, in terrible agony for everyone to see.

A large crowd of **people** watched him there, some were crying, some were **frightened**, some laughed and others just weren't sure what they should do. It took Jesus six hours to die - and when he did, everything went dark rather like an awful thunderstorm. The **soldiers** guarding him stabbed him in the side, to make sure he was dead, then they took out the **nails**, took him down and buried him in a tomb made out of solid rock.

The Easter Story - Part Two - Sunday

Tomb - Shiver and rub arms   **Wrong** - "Oh oh!"   **Dark** - Cover eyes
Cried/Crying - Wipe eyes on sleeve   **Running** - Out of breath
Morning - Alarm clock sound   **News** - Say: "What?!" and look amazed

It was very early on Sunday **morning** when Mary first woke up. She opened her eyes but couldn't see much because everything was still **dark**. She quickly got up and dressed, then left the house and started walking to the garden where Jesus was buried in the **tomb**. Everywhere was still very **dark**, and no one was around, but she wanted to go to the **tomb** to see the body of Jesus. She felt very tired and very lonely. She **cried** a little as she walked along, and she wondered how Peter was feeling that **morning**. He hadn't slept for three days, so she had been told. He was staying with John, she was glad about that.

Something was **wrong**, she noticed it as soon as she got inside the garden; the stone covering the **tomb** had fallen over, or it had been pushed away. She wondered if someone had stolen the body and she panicked. She fled out of the garden and went **running** to John's house. Peter and John were not too happy about her coming so early, but as soon as they heard the **news** they went **running** to the garden. John got there first, but he didn't go in, Peter did, and all he found was the cloth that they had wrapped Jesus in - the body was gone! Something was very **wrong**...

Peter and John went **running** back to find the others, but Mary stayed outside the **tomb**. What a terrible day! She **cried** and **cried** as she thought about it all. Just then she saw something move inside the **tomb**, she was a little frightened for it was still very **dark**, but she slowly looked in - there were two men inside the **tomb**!
One of them said, "Why are you **crying**?"

So Mary told them that someone had stolen the body, she wondered if these two men had done it but before she could ask she heard more footsteps behind her. There was a third man there, and she jumped.
"Why are you **crying**? Who are you looking for?" the man asked.

Mary just said, "If you have taken him, tell me where he is, please!"
At that point the man smiled and Mary stood very still. He called out her name, and it suddenly hit her. This man hadn't taken Jesus away - he was Jesus! She ran towards him, laughing and **crying** and talking all at the same time - she was so amazed to see him alive.

After that the rest of the morning was very confusing. Mary went back and found the others and made lots of trips to the garden to show them all that Jesus was alive. Peter came back again to have another look, but still could not work out what was going on. The men in the **tomb** were angels and they had a busy **morning** making sure everyone heard the **news**.
+ told them the news

What was the **news**? Jesus was alive!
_is_

Pentecost Day

This is more of a simple sketch than a response story, but the actions are so simple that an audience or congregation could easily follow and copy the actions if led by a group of three or four people up the front as the narrative is read out. You might like to use more than one reader. Alternatively you could rehearse it with a group of four or more people and present it as a sketch.

One day, in Jerusalem, a group of people met **together**
Squeeze together
They had stuck by one another, whatever the **weather**.
Look up check for rain
When things had gone bad, when things had been **good**
Thumbs up
They had stuck by each other as only good **friends** could
Pat each on the back

But now their best friend had gone **away**
Wave goodbye
And they weren't sure what to do when they met that **day**.
All shrug
They talked and they listened and they prayed and had a **rest**
Lean on one another
But they weren't too sure just what to do **next**.
All look at watches

Then they heard a loud noise, it sounded like a gale was **hitting**
Cover ears with hands
And little flames of fire came into the room where they were **sitting**.
Hold onto seat
The flames landed on them but they didn't get **burned**
Make flickering flame with hands
They started to talk in languages that they'd never even **heard**.
Listen and look surprised

They went out in the street saw lots of people **everywhere**
Look around, hands above eyes
And though they were lots of strangers, they didn't feel **scared**.
Look brave
They started saying things, and everyone could **hear**.
Put hand to ear
And soon there was a crowd of people lending them an **ear**.
Point to ear

Well the day went on and people's lives were **changed**.
Turn round on the spot
It was the birthday of the church and things would **never** be the same.
Shake heads
Ever since then the church has spread and **spread**
Mime spreading jam on toast
And we're here today because of what those people **did**.
Jump up and punch the air

The Dashing Prince

Princess - Flutter eyelids, saying "Flutter, flutter!" **Uncle** - HISSSS!
Heart - "Boom boom!"   **Horse** - Sound of hooves
Weetabix - "Yummy!"

This is a pantomime-style story which takes the theme of captivity and rescue. It can be used just as a piece of fun, or applied in the context of Jesus coming to rescue us from sin. You might like to try telling other stories in this OTT fashion.

This is another piece which could be acted out by a group as the story is told, and you could still have the audience doing the appropriate responses while the action unfolds.

Once upon a time there was a dashing prince - who had everything he wanted. He was popular, handsome, sporty and rich. But he was also very sad - because he was lonely.

And the reason he was lonely was because he had lost the girl of his dreams. She was a **princess** - beautiful, happy, witty and also very rich. They had been inseparable - forever together. Until one day she had run off to stay with her wicked **uncle** in the land of Scumcity. She had never come back and the dashing prince's **heart** had sunk to his boots, and broken into 23 pieces. Every day he paced up and down waiting for her - waiting, waiting - pacing, pacing - waiting and pacing - pacing and waiting - until he could take it no longer. He picked up the pieces of his broken **heart**, put them in a carrier bag and leapt off in search of his beautiful, happy, witty, rich **princess**.

The girl's wicked **uncle** was very, very, very wicked - he often growled at people, pulled faces at them and even sent them to Coventry.

He had thrown the **princess** into his castle, where he forced her to watch Neighbours and only fed her on dry **Weetabix** and instant tea. He was very horrible.

Suddenly - in the middle of our story - there came the sound of a **horse**. It was the dashing prince - pretending to be a **horse**.

He came to the castle, threw himself at the front door - and hurt his shoulder rather badly.

He shouted threats like: "Let me in!" and "Have you got a bandage for my shoulder?"

But the wicked **uncle** wasn't scared - and anyway he didn't have a first aid box. He shouted: "Go away." and "I don't talk to Jehovah's Witnesses."

Just then the beautiful, happy, witty, rich **princess** screamed.

And it made the other two jump. In fact the prince leapt up so high that he headed straight through the **princess's** window and landed in her arms.

"Oh dashing prince!" she said.

"That's me!" said the dashing prince. And while they were exchanging pleasantries the wicked **uncle** crept up behind them and bopped the prince on the head. The prince bravely fell to the floor. The **uncle** laughed. The **princess** howled. But just as it seemed that all was lost - the prince leapt up, back to life, and before the wicked **uncle** could say "*Have another dry Weetabix…*" the prince had hit him with his carrier bag and hurled him to the floor.

"Ow!" said the wicked **uncle**.

"I am here to save you." The prince said.

"Do you mind if I just finish my dry **Weetabix**?" The **princess** said.

She had obviously had a very traumatic time! But the dashing prince took her hand, her arm, and every bit of her, flung her on the **horse** and rescued her from the wicked **uncle** and his evil kingdom. Then he took her back home where they all lived happily ever after.

The Starfish

Starfish - Flick out fingers of both hands, like stars
Beach - Dust sand off hands   **Difference** - Snap fingers
Millions - Look amazed

An old man was walking along the **beach** one day, very early in the morning, when he saw a young man ahead of him picking up **starfish** and flinging them into the sea. Catching up with the young man he asked him what he was doing.

"The **starfish** will die if they are still on the **beach** when the sun comes up - it will be too hot for them," the young man said.
"But the **beach** goes on for miles and there are **millions** of **starfish**," replied the old man, "what good can you do? How can your little effort make any **difference**?"

The young man looked at the little **starfish** in his hand then smiled and threw it safely into the waves.
"Yes," he said, "there are **millions** - and I can't make a **difference** to all of them... But I can make a **difference** to this one."

And with that he walked on, picking up another **starfish** as he went.

Making Waves

Stone - "Ouch!"   **Puddle** - Make a "pop" by flicking finger in mouth
Waves - Wave hands   **Splash** - Brush water off face and clothes

The old man picked up a **stone** and dropped it into the **puddle**. There was a very large **splash**, and our clothes got wet. Then, as we watched, one ripple after another drifted out across the **puddle** to its edges. I took a little piece of gravel and threw that in, it didn't make a big **splash**, but once again lots of little rings of water spread out across the **puddle**.

All morning we played the game, me and that old man, big **stones** and little **stones**, gravel and rocks; **stone** after **stone** we tossed them into the **puddle**, and every time those little **waves** spread out across the surface. And when we dropped two **stones** in at once the **waves** hit each other, and made other shapes and different patterns.

Eventually the old man sat back on the bench and lit his pipe.
"Everything we do and everything we say is like one of those **stones**," he said, "it sends out little **waves**, little signals which affect other people and change their lives. We can't help it. Some people like to make a big **splash** and some people only make a little **splash**, but all of us make **waves**, and those **waves** affect other people; sometimes for good, sometimes for bad." He nodded his head slowly. "So I think everyone should think very carefully about the sort of **waves** they want to make."

I thought about that for a while, then decided what to do. I put my feet together, jumped as high as I could into the air and landed like a very big **stone** in the **puddle**. The **splash** I made was huge and it went everywhere - but the **waves** that I made went even further...

The Ship

Sand - Smooth hands over imaginary sand   **Friend** - Clasp hands
Sea/Ocean - Make waves with arms
Anchor - Mime pulling up anchor
Sail/Sails/Sailing - Place hands in front of face and blow like sails

This story is based on a simple parable about losing those we love.

The little girl [or boy] sat on a rock by the **sea**. She was crying and the tears were falling quickly onto the **sand**. She had lost a **friend** - a **friend** she thought would never leave her. A **friend** she thought she could trust to always be there. But now she was gone. Gone forever.

As she looked at the **sea** she saw a large, beautiful **sailing** ship standing in the bay. It was raising its **anchor**, ready to begin its long journey across the **ocean**. The wind buffeted the **sails** into life and it begin to move away from the **sea**shore, away from the girl, away from the tears in the **sand**.

The girl stopped crying as she watched the white fluttering **sails** melt into the creamy marshmallow clouds, and she had to screw up her eyes to keep watching it as it became just a tiny white speck - then vanished over the horizon. Just then a little boy ran past with his father and their dog.
"Look! It's gone, it's gone!" said the boy, pointing out to **sea**.
His father only laughed and walked on.

"Gone?" thought the little girl, "gone? No, it hasn't gone - we just can't see it anymore, but soon other people will be able to see it. Soon it will **sail** up to another shore and other children will stand on the **sand** and watch it **sail** in. And they'll shout: '*Here it comes, here it comes...*'"

And the little girl thought again of her **friend**, gone forever - yet not gone. Disappeared from the girl's life only to arrive at a new place, a new world, a new **sandy** beach where others would watch her come, and then they too would shout excitedly: "*Here she is... here she is...*"

Telling *More* Tales

INDEX

Other Stories

Creation

Dark - *Screw up eyes*   **Blew** - *Blow noisily*
Dust - *Scoop up dust and let it fall through flicking fingers*
Stretch - *Mime stretching some plasticine with hands, and make appropriate noise*   **Flashing** - *Flick fingers*
Mirror - *Breathe on & polish an imaginary mirror*
Set fire - *Whoosh!*   **Light** - *Open eyes wide*

In the beginning everywhere was very dark.
There was only God and people had not been invented.
God shouted very loud, "Let there be **light**!" And suddenly the **darkness** became **light**.
Then God took a handful of **dust** and sprinkled it about and **blew** on it, the **dust** became millions of tiny stars **flashing** all across the universe.
Then God **blew** into his hands and made a big ball of air, he **blew** and **blew** and **blew** until the ball was as big as the sun then he let it float into the sky and he **set fire** to it. That was the sun.
Next God made the moon, it was like a big **mirror.** He took another big ball of air and polished it until it shone and you could see your face in it. Just like a **mirror.** Then he took the **mirror** and hung it in the sky opposite the sun.
God made lots of planets and hung them all over the sky. Then he made one called Earth and he beamed himself down onto it, and landed in a garden. There was a lot of soil and **dust** there, so God took a handful of the **dust**, **blew** onto it and then began to **stretch** it out like a huge piece of plasticine. He **stretched** and **stretched** it until it was big enough to make it into the shape of a person. So that's what he did, he made a man, **blew** on him, and the man woke up. Then God took some more **dust**, **stretched** it into a different shape and made a woman. The man and woman and God became very good friends, and that was how it all began.

Cain and Abel

Cain - One side stand up quickly then sit down again
Abel - Other side stand up
Animals - All make different animal sounds
Lambs - Say "Baaa!"   **Angry** - "Grrr!"
Food - "Chomp chomp chomp!"
Water - "Slurp!"   **Vegetables** - "Yummy!"
Squelchy - "Ugh!"   **Smelly** - "Poo!"

Adam and Eve had two sons. One was called **Cain**, the other **Abel**.
Abel was good with **animals**. He loved them and was good at looking after them. He fed them, he gave them water, he protected them, and he
Cain, on the other hand wasn't so good with **animals**. He was better with **vegetables**, **vegetables** didn't run around like **animals**. They didn't make as much **noise** and they didn't leave large piles of dung for you to step in.
One day, at Harvest time, **Cain** decided to bring some of his **vegetables** to God, as a thank you for all that he'd been able to grow.
Abel saw this and decided to bring a **lamb** to God. The Bible tells us that God accepted **Abel**'s **lamb** and was very pleased with it.
But not **Cain**'s **vegetables**. Perhaps they were off, perhaps they were moldy, perhaps they were **smelly** and **squelchy**. We don't know, but we do know that **Cain** was not very pleased about it. Not very pleased about it at all, in fact he was very, very, very **angry**. Very **angry** indeed.
Abel meanwhile went back to his other lambs and gave them food and water.
Then, one day, **Cain** said to **Abel**, "Let's go for a nice, quiet peaceful walk."
And while they were out **Cain** picked up one of his prize **vegetables** and hit **Abel** with it. He hit him so hard that **Abel** never got up again. Then he ran away. But when God found out about it he was very **angry**. And so he told **Cain** off and told him to move away and live in a different place. Poor old **Cain** but God promised to look after him at least he was alive and well, not like his brother **Abel**.

The Big Tower

Language/s - "Rabbit, rabbit!"   **Big** - Stretch out arms wide
Tower - Look up   **Idea** - Slap hand to head
Hammering - "Bang! Bang!"   **Sawing** - "Zzz! Zzz!"

Sometimes we get an **idea**, and think it's great, but it may not be, if it's something we try and do all on our own.

There was a time, a long, long, time ago, when everybody spoke the same **language.** And they all had a big chat together one day and decided to build a **big** city and in the city there would be a big **tower**, so **big** that it would touch the sky.

"This will be a very good **idea**," they all said. "It will be just what we need to bring us all **together**."

So they set to work, **hammering,** and **sawing, sawing** and **hammering.** And before long the city began to take shape. It was very **big,** and full of **big** buildings and roads. And of course, there was the very, very **big tower**, reaching on up to the sky.

Now one day, God came down and went for a walk in the city. He looked around at all the new things, the roads and buildings and **tower**, and he was sad.

He was sad because the people were doing it all themselves and hadn't asked for his help.

So he said, "I think I'd better do something to stop people getting so confident that they think they can live without my help. And as he stood listening, he heard voices, and he heard the people all talking the same **language.** And he clicked his fingers and said, "That's what I'll do, I'll give them all a different **language,** so that they can't understand each other anymore, and then they won't be able to keep **hammering,** and **sawing** anymore because they'll be too mixed up."

So God worked a miracle and gave different people different **languages, just** like we have today and they had to stop building the big **city** and the **big tower.** And instead they started to spread all over the world, to different countries, with their different **languages** and their **tower** wasn't such a **big idea** after all.

Moses and the Burning Bush

Hot - Fan face with hand
Fire - "Crackle hiss! Crackle hiss!"
Suddenly - Sharp intake of breath and lean back
Shoes - Stamp feet   **Bored** - Do a big yawn
Can't - Shake heads   **Can** - Nod
Pharaoh - Do a quick Egyptian sand dance

Now, Moses was a shepherd. He worked out in the desert where it was very **hot**, so **hot** that things would often catch **fire**. Trees and plants would sometimes often **suddenly** burst into flames, it was so **hot**.

Now one day Moses was out in the desert, looking after his sheep, as he always did. He'd done the same job for forty years, so he was very good at it. But he was also a bit **bored** with it, and a bit fed up because a long time ago he had once lived in a palace, and now he only had a tent. And he had once   had a nice easy life, but now he had to work hard every day, he had eaten the best food, and had slaves to keep him cool, but now he was always **hot**.

Then one day, as he was out in the desert withe sheep, feeling a little **bored**, he was about to hang his coat on a nearby bush when **suddenly** - it caught **fire**! Just like that! He was about to run away when he noticed something, the bush was on **fire** but it wasn't getting burnt. Not at all. So he went to take a closer look, and then he heard it. A voice.

It said, "Take off your **shoes**."

So he did.

There was an angel inside the burning bush, an angel sent by God.

Moses heard the voice say, "This is a very special place, God is here and it's very holy."

At that Moses dropped onto his knees and covered up his face, for he was afraid to look at God.

Then God said to Moses, "I've got a job for you. I want you to help the Israelites."

But Moses said, "I've already got a job."

So God said, "Well I've got another on now. I want you to go and see **Pharaoh**."

"But I **can't**," said Moses.

"Oh yes you **can**," said God.

"Oh no I **can't**."

"Oh yes you **can**."

"Oh no I **can't**."

"Oh yes you **can**."

Well it went on for quite a while like this, and Moses didn't want to go because he knew what a mess he'd made of things in the past.

But in the end God told him he could take his brother along and so Moses accepted the job, put his **shoes** back on and went back to Egypt and confronted **Pharaoh**. After that he was never **bored** again!

Gideon's Selection Process

This is not so much a response story, more a way of including the whole congregation in the Bible story. The aim is that they should experience what Gideon's men experienced as their numbers were whittled down.

Ask everyone to stand up and explain that you would like their help with a dramatic version of a Bible story. As you are about to begin reading the passage, stop, think then announce that it is something particularly for the adults so anyone under 15 may sit down. Look as if you are about to read again then stop, think again, and announce that anyone wearing ear rings may sit down. Think again then say that anyone who had cornflakes for breakfast may sit, anyone who has read a newspaper today, anyone with blue eyes... You may like to add your own, particularly if you want to fix the exercise so that one particular person is left standing! Anyway, when you have eventually narrowed the congregation down to one or perhaps two people, call them out and give them the following passage to read.

Gideon defeats the Midianites.
The Lord said to Gideon, 'The men you have are too many for me to give them victory over the Midianites. They might think that they had won by themselves, and so give me no credit. Announce to the people, "Anyone who is afraid should go back home..."'
So twenty two thousand went back, but ten thousand stayed.
Then the Lord said to Gideon, 'You still have too many men. Take them down to the water, and I will separate them for you there. If I tell you a man should go with you, he will go...'
There were three hundred men who scooped up water in their hands and lapped it; all the others got down on their knees to drink.
The Lord said to Gideon, 'I will rescue and give you victory over the Midianites with the three hundred men who lapped the water. Tell everyone else to go home.'

Judges 7 v 2-3, 4, 6-7

Balaam and the Donkey

Bed - "Creak! Creak!"
Desert - Make sound of wind gusting across the sand
Quick - Clap hands twice   **Money** - "Ooooh!"
Zoomed - "Neeeow!"   **Donkey** - "Ee aw!"

Once there was a king who lived a long time ago. His name was king Balak. One day he woke up, got out of **bed**, looked out of his royal window and got a shock. He saw thousands and thousands of Israelites coming towards his town across the **desert**.
"**Quick**!" he said. "Go and get Balaam. He's a real cool prophet who will help me get rid of these invading Israelites."
So he sent off some of his people to go and bring Balaam back. When they saw Balaam they offered him a lot of **money** and asked him to go back with them and curse the Israelites.
Balaam said he'd have to think about it, so they all went to **bed**. In the middle of the night God woke Balaam up and said, "Who are these people who have come to visit you?"
Balaam told God about the **money** and the Israelites and the **desert**.
"Don't go," said God. "These Israelites are my favourite people and I don't want you going and causing trouble for them."
So the next day Balaam said he couldn't go and the people **zoomed** back to King Balak.
When King Balak heard this he said, "**Quick**! Go back and offer him more **money**!"
So the men went and offered Balaam more **money**.
Balaam said he couldn't do it, but later when they had all gone to **bed**, God told Balaam he could go with them to see Balak, as long as he did exactly what God told to and nothing else.
Balaam was really excited now as the king had offered him an awful lot of money, to the next morning, **quick** as a flash, he **zoomed** out of **bed**, saddled up his **donkey**, and went off with the others back to King Balak.

On the way the **donkey** suddenly bolted and **zoomed** off the road, so Balaam had to go and drag her back. Then a bit further along the **donkey** did another strange thing, she pressed herself against a wall as they rode along and crushed Balaam's foot. Last of all she lay down in the road and refused to budge at all.

"What's going on!" yelled Balaam at his **donkey** and then, surprise surprise, the **donkey** began to talk.

"Why are you mad at me?" she said. "I've just   saved your life three times."

And then an angel appeared in the road, carrying a huge sword.

"You've got a very smart **donkey**," said the angel, "I've come to kill you because you were in such a hurry to go to King Balak for **money**. If you're **donkey** hadn't been so **quick** when she saw me, you'd be mincemeat and raspberry jam now. Balaam, you must do what God says, you mustn't just go and see Balak for the **money**, you must go because God   sends you."

And so Balaam went and instead of cursing the Israelites he blessed them, and King Balak was not a happy man. But Balaam was **quick** to obey God, and he was very glad that the **donkey** had saved his life.

Saul's Narrow Escape

Jealous - Cross arms and look moody
Kill - Sharp intake of breath "Haaa!" and put hand on chest
Hide - Cover head with hands and stoop down out of sight
Creep/Crept - Strike a stealthy top toeing pose and freeze this
Sword - "Clank!"
Loo - Mime bashing on door and shout "Hurry up!"
Cave - "Hello, hello, hello, hello..." Fading away like an echo

King Saul had once been a good king, but as he got older he went off the rails a bit. He and David had once been good friends but now Saul was very **jealous** of him and he wanted to **kill** David. So David had to **hide** out in a **cave** out in the desert.

One day, as Saul was out searching for David to try and **kill** him, he went into a **cave** to go to the **loo**.
But he didn't realise that David was **hiding** in that very **cave**. And when David saw Saul **creep** inside on his way to use the **loo**, David thought to himself, "Now's my chance, I can **kill** Saul and then he won't be able to **kill** me."

So David **crept** forward in the darkness and lifted up his **sword.** Saul didn't see him and now David had the perfect chance to **kill** him. But as he stood there, **sword** in hand, David changed his mind, he knew that   God had once chosen Saul to be king, and even though Saul was **jealous** of David and wanted to **kill** him, that didn't mean that David should do the same to Saul. So instead, David took his **sword** and sliced off the bottom of Saul's cloak, and then he **crept** away, back into the darkness of the **cave.**

When Saul turned round and left the **cave** David followed him outside and shouted to him, "My lord, the king," and he bowed down to Saul. Then he said, "Look at your cloak, I was **hiding** in that **cave** when I saw you **creep** in, I could have **killed** you, but I didn't, if you don't believe me, look at your cloak, it's a bit shorter that it used to be!"

Then Saul realised the truth and he began to cry.

"You're a better man than me," he said, "I was **jealous** of you, but you had the chance to **kill** me with your **sword** and you didn't. Thank you for not punishing me, thank you for being kind. One day God will make you king and reward you for what you've done today."

And after that Saul went home, and David went back to his **cave**.

A Time for Everything

This is a more of a 'copy sketch' than a response story, i.e. one person reads the narrative and another person, or group of people, leads the congregation in simple mimed responses.

There is a time for everything.	*Hold out hands wide*
A time for babies to be born.	*Cradle a baby in arms*
A time for people to die.	*Look sad, bow head*
A time to plant things in the garden.	*Mime digging*
A time to dig them up again.	*Mime more digging*
A time to kill.	*Slap fly on shoulder*
A time to heal.	*Put plaster on knee*
A time to knock things down.	*Mime swinging a sledge hammer*
A time to build them up again.	*Pile up blocks on top of the other*
A time for crying.	*Wipe a tear from eye*
A time for laughing.	*Mime laughing, hold sides*
A time for feeling sad.	*Put on a sad face*
A time for feeling happy.	*Change to a happy face*
A time for scattering things.	*Throw hands out scattering seeds*
A time for collecting them up again.	*Mime collecting seeds up again*
A time to hug.	*Embrace a real or invisible person*
A time not to hug.	*Step away from them*
A time to find something.	*Pick up something very tiny*
A time to lose it again.	*Look at empty hand and look around*
A time for keeping things.	*Put something in pocket*
A time for throwing them away.	*Pull out and throw away*
A time to rip things up.	*Mime ripping a sheet of paper*
A time to put them back together.	*Join the bits up again*
A time to be quiet.	*Put fingers to lips saying "Shh!"*
A time to shout out loud.	*Put hands to wide mouth, shouting*
A time for loving and caring.	*Blow a kiss*
A time for not loving and caring.	*Slap a hand over mouth*
A time for war.	*Make fists and look threatening*
A time for peace.	*Relax, lean on hands behind head*

No Need to Fight

Jehoshaphat – "Bless you!"
Pray - Look amazed and wide-eyed   **King** - All bow
Fight - One side fire arrows, other side swing swords
Rescue operation - Cheer very loudly   **Bad guys** - Look mean and sneer

Back in the days when everyone in Jerusalem worshipped God, they had a **king** who had a very funny name. He was called **Jehoshaphat**. It was an unusual name and he was a most unusual **king**. Because **Jehoshaphat** - he was a very good **king**, and he encouraged all the people to obey God.

Now one day **Jehoshaphat** found out that all his people were going to be attacked. Now he could have got everyone to join the army, or he could have gone to some of the other countries for help. But no, **Jehoshaphat** did something else. He went to God. He told everybody that they must **pray** about the problem and see what God would do. They also went without food for a while to help them **pray.**

After they had prayed God spoke to them and he said   "You won't have to **fight** this battle. Not at all. This battle is mine, not yours. All you have to do is go out there, take your position and watch me perform an amazing **rescue operation.**"

The army coming to attack them was very large indeed, so it was quite scary to go and do what   God had told them but **Jehoshaphat** knew that he could trust God to do what he had promised.

So, early the next morning **Jehoshaphat** led his people outside and told them all that they weren't going to **fight**, instead they were going to sing songs of praise to God. And though this was not the usual way to **fight** a battle the people did as they were told because they knew **Jehoshaphat** was a good **king**.

Well, the **bad guys** came closer and closer and there was an awful lot of them, then, just as they were about to attack, **Jehoshaphat** told everyone to sing praises to God, and as they did the bad guys got completely mixed up and started fighting each other! Amazing! And before too long a lot of the **bad guys** were dead, and the rest ran away and **Jehoshaphat** and all the people praised the Lord that he had done an amazing **rescue operation** and kept them safe from the **bad guys**.

What Jesus Did For Us

Wrote - Mime writing in the air
Feel/Felt - Place hand on chest and beat twice, like a heartbeat
Run - Sound of running feet
Silent - Place hand over mouth
Wander - Cover eyes with one hand and grope the air with other hand
Rejected - Mime pushing someone away
Friends - Punch the air and say "Yes!"

Eight hundred years before Jesus was born there was a man called Isaiah, and he **wrote** about the things that Jesus would do for us. This is what he **wrote**:

There was a man who was like a tender green shoot, growing up in a bit of old dry waste ground.

We didn't think there was anything interesting about him so we **rejected** him and pushed him away.

That made him **feel** all the things we often **feel**, he **felt** hurt he **felt** upset and he **felt** left out and **rejected**.

And he knew what it was like when everyone turns away from you and you're left on your own.

So he experienced all those things that hurt us, along with all the things that weigh us down and make us **feel** bad.

And God **punished** him because of all the thing we do wrong, even though it wasn't his fault.

He was **punished** for our crimes and our mistakes and our selfishness.

He suffered a lot of pain so that he could make us better.

We all often **wander** away from God and do our own thing, yet God pointed the finger at him, not us. We **wander** away on our own schemes and ideas and yet God told him off, not us.

Like an innocent animal, killed for no reason, he was murdered.

Yet he never argued or complained or tried to escape or run **away**. Not at all. He stayed **silent**.

He stood there and took it all.

He didn't **run** off, he let people do bad things to him. He let them say he was a criminal and he let them put him in prison and then he let them kill him. And no one realised that it was us who should have been **punished**, because he didn't say that, he didn't speak up, he was **silent** and he let himself be **punished** and **rejected** instead, in our place.

And afterwards, when he was dead, he was buried in a rich man's grave.

But that wasn't the end, after **feeling** all that pain and going through all of these problems, he came back to life again.

And because of all this, many people will be forgiven and become **friends** with God.

And many people will have a new start in life.

Looking Ahead

Difficult - Bite on knuckles
Plans - Mime unrolling a scroll
Worry - Look scared
Happy - Put on a big smile
Heart - Place hand on heart
Strength - Hold up arms in strong man pose

One day God spoke to his people and said:
You might be having problems and things might be really **difficult** sometimes.
But I'm the only one who knows all about the **plans** I have for you.
And I have some very good **plans** for you.
I know what the future looks like and it looks hopeful.
Don't **worry** about the past, because my name is not I was.
Don't **worry** about the future, because my name is not I will be.
My name, said God, is I am. I'm here in the present.
So just try and focus on today and trust me.

Try and settle down where you are, try and be **happy** with all you have, even when things are **difficult** and keep looking to me.
I have good **plans** for you, and when you pray to me, I will listen.
And when you look for me I will be there.
Get to know me with all your **heart** and **strength** and then we will be really good friends.
And when you search for me you will find me.
So trust me with all your **heart** and all your **strength**, and try not to **worry** when things get **difficult**.

Neville's Christmas

The Christmas story, as told to Neville and his friends on the river.

Neville - Say : "Rrribbit rrribbit!"
Christmas - Sing: "Jingle bells" or "Ding ding merrily on high"
Paper - "Rrippp!"   **Presents** - "Oooohh!"
Lights - "Twinkle twinkle!"   **Baby** - Say: "Aaah!"
Food - "Mmmm!" Rub stomach and lick lips
Shepherds - Sniff and wipe nose with back of hand

Neville the little green frog loved **Christmas**.
It was full of glossy **paper**, and ribbons, and **presents**, and rich custard with pudding. He loved the smell of **Christmas** trees and cold nights, and the colours from the bright **lights** and late night shopping.

His favourite time was **Christmas** morning, when all the animals on the river bank would tumble round to Toad's house and open their **presents** amidst the flurry of tearing sellotape, bulging parcels, shouts of surprise and mugs of refreshing, hot tea. Then, when the **presents** were all opened, and the wrapping **paper** sat high in one corner like a little **paper** mount Everest, then Toad would sit happily back in his big armchair and tell them about the first **Christmas**. About the long, dark night as Joseph and Mary travelled to Bethlehem; it was such a long, hard journey, and poor Mary had felt quite ill because she was soon to have her **baby**. Then Toad would describe the inn - that beautiful hotel, glittering with warmth and soft **lights**, offering good **food** and comfy chairs. But Joseph and Mary never saw the inside, because the place was full, and the innkeeper only shook his head.

Then Mary and Joseph crept around the back, and the innkeeper let them sleep in his old, damp, crumbling stable - and that was where Mary had her beautiful child. The most important **baby** in the world, yet he was born outside because there just wasn't room anywhere else.

And then Toad's eyes would **light** up - and he would talk about the **shepherds**, running madly down the hill, faster and faster, not stopping until they had rushed into the stable and almost tripped over the **baby** as it lay in the animals' food stall. Those **shepherds** looked in amazement - and they laughed and cried, and shouted and then knelt and prayed in front of the **baby**.

Why? Because they knew something that only God could tell them - they knew that this **baby** was Jesus Christ, the perfect Son of God. And then... the **shepherds** leapt up again and ran back up the hill for a cup of tea.

And then Toad would yawn, and tell them all it was time for his afternoon nap, even though it was still only 7 o'clock in the morning; and so Neville, and Otto, and Ferdinand, and all the other animals on the river bank would creep off and play their **Christmas** games, and eat their **Christmas food**, and think about that special **Christmas baby**...

Shepherds and Kings

Baby - Hold baby and look shocked
Decree - Stamp fist of one hand on the flat of another
Straw - "Poo!" Hold nose   **Sky** - Sweep hands out above head
Sore - "Ouch"   **Tired** - Stretch
Back - Indicate over shoulder with thumb

Jesus was born in Bethlehem
At a time long ago way **back** when
Caesar was in charge and he issued a **decree**
He said, "I want to know how many people are under me."

So everyone had to go to their place of birth
So a young couple came from Nazareth.
The **decree** said "Go" so they travelled all day
And when they arrived there was nowhere to stay.

They found an inn and knocked on the door
The owner was **tired** and his head was **sore**.
They said, "We've come to give Caesar our autograph."
And the innkeeper said, "There's a room round the **back.**"

Round the **back** of the place they found a cave
There was no soft bed and nowhere to shave.
There was just smelly **straw** and spiders and mice
And when the couple saw it they had to think twice.

The innkeeper said, "It's the only place free.
Everywhere's full 'cause of Caesar's **decree.**"
The couple took the place and they spent the night
They were **tired,** and sore, but they made it through all right.

The couple were called Mary and Joe
And when the morning came they had a **baby** in tow.
Mary gave birth in the middle of the night.
In the **straw** and the dung, it was quite a sight.

Some shepherds came by to wet the **baby's** head.
They were quite amazed - this is what they said,
"We saw angels in the **sky** and they sang us a song.
They said, "Peace on earth, and hope for everyone."

The **baby** grew a little and some men dropped by
They'd followed a star way up in the **sky.**
The men were rich and they'd bought presents.
Gold and myrrh and frankincense.

Everyone knew when they came to see
This was no ordinary pregnancy.
This **baby** had come to change the planet
And way **back** then, that was how God began it.

A Visit to the Temple

Temple - "Shhh!" as if respecting the quiet there
Celebration - Shout "Yippee!"
Lost - Slap hand on forehead and say "Oh no!"
Mum - Look up and to right
Dad - Look up and to left
Son - Hold out hand to show height of Jesus as a boy

When Jesus was twelve his **mum** and **dad** took him to the **temple**. It wasn't like going to church when you can just hop in the car and zoom down the road. They had to travel for **miles** and **miles** on foot, walking for several days. The **temple** was in Jerusalem, a big city full of life and people.

There was a big **celebration** there called the Passover festival. This was a **celebration** to remember how God rescued their families from Egypt hundreds of years ago.

"Stay close to us," Jesus **mum** and **dad** told him. "And don't get **lost**."

They stayed in Jerusalem for the festival and then they all packed their bags, left the **temple** and headed for home. When they stopped at the end of the first day's travelling Jesus's **mum** looked around and couldn't find him anywhere. She went and told his **dad** and they looked all about but it seemed that Jesus wasn't with them. He had got **lost**.

"We'll have to go back to the **temple**," said his **mum** and his **dad** agreed.

So they turned around and walked for **miles** and **miles** and **miles** back to the **temple**.

The **celebrations** were still going on when they arrived back in Jerusalem.

They looked in the streets and in the shops and in the houses but Jesus was nowhere to be seen.

"I hope he's not been kidnapped," said his **mum.**

"He must be in the **temple**," said his **dad.**

They went inside and saw a very large crowd of wise men sitting on the floor listening to a very wise teacher.

"Let's ask them," said his **mum**.

They tip toed over and tapped one of the men on the shoulder.

"Excuse me," said Jesus's **dad.** "Have you seen our **son**? He's called Jesus."

The man didn't say a word he just pointed to the centre of the circle. There sitting in the middle was their young **son**, talking while everyone else sat listening. Mary and Joseph were amazed.

"Where've you been?" said Mary. "We've been looking everywhere for you."

Jesus smiled. "Didn't you guess I would be here?" he said. "This is my father's house."

Mary knew that he wasn't talking about Joseph, his **dad**, he was talking about God, his real father. And so, having found their **son** safe and sound, they all left the **temple** and went home.

A Tempting Time

First - Hole up one finger and shout "One"
Second - Hold up two fingers and shout "Two"
Third - Hold up three fingers and shout "Three"
Fourth - Hold up four fingers and shout "Four"
Rocks - Make a fist as if it's a rock and beat it on other palm
Wild Animals - Make wild animal sounds
Words - Blow gently onto open hand and press hand against heart

Before Jesus could begin his work he had to go through a series of challenges.

First:

He went out into the wilderness where he had to survive all on on his own, with no one else around.

Second:

He had no food and he was out there for forty days so he felt very weak and hungry by the end of that time.

Third:

There were **wild animals** out there, and he had to trust God to keep him safe.

Fourth:

He had to face three difficult tests.

The **first** was this. He was tempted to turn the **rocks** around him into lovely soft fresh bread. As he was very hungry this was a very difficult test. He could easily have done it with all the power that   he had, he could have turned the **rocks** into all kinds of delicious food, but he didn't, instead he remembered these **words**. "It takes more than bread to stay alive - we need to have God's life giving **words**."

The **second** test was this. He found himself on top of the temple in the city and was tempted to make a spectacular jump so that God would send some angels to catch him so that he wouldn't even stub his toe on the **rocks** below. People in the city would see it and it would prove that he was the Son of God and that he couldn't die yet, because he had a very special mission to do. Jesus remembered these **words**, "Whatever you do don't test God, trust him."

The **third** test happened like this. He walked up onto the **rocks** overlooking miles and miles of beautiful cities. And a voice said to him, "You can have all this. All of it, you can be in charge of it all. All you have to do is worship me instead of God."

Jesus could have had all the power in the world over the cities and the people in them. They would have been under his control. It was very tempting, but instead Jesus said, "Worship God, he is the Lord of heaven and earth and he is the only one we must ever worship."

Jesus knew that he already had all the power in the world he didn't have to prove it by leaping off those **rocks**. After this God sent his angels to look after Jesus and keep him safe from the **wild animals**.

The Pearl and the Treasure

Field - Divide into two sides, side 1: "Squelch!",
then side 2: "Splat!", 1: "Squelch!", 2: "Splat!"
Tripped - "Oops!"
Soil - Rub fingers together as if feeling mud and soil, say "Ooh lovely!"
Chest - Stagger under the weight of the chest you are miming holding
Pearl - Breathe on pearl and hold it up
Treasure - Throw handfuls of jewels in the air and look amazed

Once there was a man who **tripped** in a **field.** He was just walking happily across it when he caught his foot, **tripped,** and fell headlong. He had a bruise on his knee and another on his arm. As he sat up and rubbed them he noticed a shiny metal corner sticking out of the **soil.** He began scraping around it, pulling the **soil** away and soon he saw that there was a metal **chest**   buried in the ground. He dug it out of the **soil** and opened up the **chest.** Inside it was full of precious stones and jewels. Hundreds of them! The more he looked the more he saw. Just then he heard a voice.

"Oi! What are you doing in my **field**?"

It was the farmer.

The man told him he wanted to buy the **field** and the **treasure,** but the farmer said it would cost him everything he had. The man said he didn't mind, so he sold his house, his car, his clothes, his CD   collection, his videos, his computer and his hamster.

When he'd bought the **field** he took the **chest** home, then remembered that he'd sold his home so he went back to the **field** and sat down in it and thought how lucky he was to have found something that was worth so much.

In the next **field** there was a tiny **pearl** buried in the **soil.** It had been there for years, just hoping that one day someone would come along and find it. But no one did, and so the **pearl** became and more unhappy. It was worth an awful lot, and was a most unusual and unique **pearl** but no one realised it and no one bothered to look for it. Then one day, a woman who collected **pearls** started searching through the **field** looking for precious stones. She dug down deep and was amazed and overjoyed to find the little **pearl.** She took it home and made a beautiful pendant with the it.

And what are these stories about? You and me. We're just like that precious **pearl,** buried in the **soil,** waiting to be found by God and his kingdom. And when we're discovered by God, then we're like the man in the first story who found the **treasure chest,** we want to give everything we've got so that we can have that very precious **treasure.**

The Weeds

Wheat - "Munch Munch"
Thistles - "Ow!"
Farmer Fred - Friendly wave: "'ello there!"
Farmer Felix - Evil laugh: "Hee hee hee!"
Pull - Reach down to the floor and give a big tug

Once there were two farmers who lived next door to each other. The first farmer was called **Farmer Fred** and he was good and kind, but the second was called **Farmer Felix** and he was nasty and naughty. Well, one day **Farmer Fred** went out and sowed some **wheat** in one of his fields. That night, when it was all dark, **Farmer Felix**, who'd been watching him, crept into the field and sowed a lot of weeds in amongst the **wheat.** Well, not long after **thistles** sprang up all over the field.

"It must be **Farmer Felix**," said **Farmer Fred**. "He's been sowing weeds in amongst my crops."

He wondered if he should try and **pull** the **thistles** out, but then he decided not to.

"I might trample on the **wheat** while I'm doing that," he said. "Instead I'll let the two grow up side by side and then I'll **pull** up the whole lot and sort out the wheat from the **thistles** then."

And that's what he did. When the time for harvesting came **Farmer Fred pulled** up the **thistles** and the **wheat.** He put the **wheat** safely into his barns and he burnt the **thistles.**

What's that story mean? Well, Jesus is like **Farmer Fred** who goes out and sows a lot of good seeds. The field is the world that is full of people, some of the people are like the **wheat** some are like the **thistles**. At the end of time Jesus and the angels will sort out the people, and like the story, the people who are like the **wheat** will go to a safe place, and those who are like the **thistles** will be destroyed.

Feeding 5000 People

Rumbling - Make a rumbling sound
Stomachs - Pat stomachs   **Food** - "Mmmmm!"
Five loaves and two little fish - Hold up five fingers, then two fingers

One day a lot of people were sitting on a hill listening to Jesus. Suddenly they heard the sound of **rumbling.** Was it an earthquake? Was it a tornado? It started very quietly and gradually got louder and louder and louder.

"What's that noise?" asked one of Jesus' friends, a man called Andrew.

"It's my **stomach,"** said a voice.

"No it's not, it's my **stomach,"** said another voice.

"Not it's not, it's my **stomach,"** said another voice.

All over the hillside **stomachs** were **rumbling** steadily. Everyone was very hungry.

"Has anyone got any **food**?" asked Andrew.

No one had. The **rumbling** continued.

"Oh dear," said Andrew, "things are looking very serious. There are thousands of people here. We could start an avalanche with all this **rumbling."**

Then a little boy stuck his hand up.

"It's okay," he said. "I've got loads of **food.** My mum gave me extra."

What a relief. Everyone perked up then.

"Bring it over here," said Andrew, so the little boy did.

"Where is it all?" asked Andrew.

"Here," said the boy and he held up a little sack.

"That!" said Andrew, "but there's only **five loaves and two little fish**."

"I don't mind sharing it," said the boy, "it's way too much for me. Way too much."

Andrew looked at the little boy who just smiled, so Andrew looked at Jesus, and he just smiled.

"You and the others can pass it round," said Jesus.

"But there's only **five loaves and two little fish**," said Andrew.

"No problem," said Jesus. "I'll just say grace."

And so he did. He blessed the food and then slowly, with terrified faces his friends broke the **five loaves and two little fish** into small pieces and began to pass round the crumbs. On and on they passed it round and the food never ran out. At the end of the day, when everyone had full **stomachs** they went round collecting up the leftovers and they had twelve baskets of **food.** The little boy's eyes nearly popped.

"I can't eat all that!" he said. "That's way too much."

"Take it home for your family then," said Andrew. "Tell them Jesus was cooking today."

And so he did.

Walking on Water

Wind - All howl   **Waves** - "Splash!"
Boat - Mime rowing hard as if in a storm
Rain/Rainy - Shake head from side to side as if shaking off raindrops
Screamed - Scream!   **Water** - "Glug glug glug!"

Just after Jesus had fed 5000 people he told his disciples to go off in their **boat** while he stayed to wave goodbye to all the people and make sure they were all okay. Then, when the people had all gone home he went up a quiet hill to be on his own and to pray.

Meanwhile, out on the lake a storm began to blow up. The **wind** grew stronger, the **waves** grew bigger, and the **rain** began to lash across the **water** and into the **boat.** The storm went on through the night and the disciples were worried the **boat** might tip over and they all might drown. Then, at four o'clock in the morning Peter pointed over the side of the **boat,** into the **rainy** darkness.

"Look!" he **screamed.** "Look!"

There was figure standing on the **waves,** doing the impossible, walking on the **water.** The disciples took one look then all **screamed.**

"Don't panic," said the figure, "it's only me."

"It's Jesus," said Peter. "It's you Lord. Tell you what, if it really is you tell me I can walk on **water** too."

"All right," said Jesus. "Step out of the **boat** and come and join me."

As the others watched Peter took one step out and placed his foot on the **waves.** Then he put his other foot out and before he knew what was happening he was standing there, right on the **water,** not sinking!

He started walking towards Jesus, and everything was going fine, then suddenly he realised what he was doing, he looked around at the **wind** and the **waves** and the **rain,** and he began to sink.

"Help! Save me!" he **screamed.**

As soon as he said this Jesus was there beside him, he stretched out his hand and pulled Peter up out of the **water.**

"Why did you doubt?" said Jesus. "You were doing so well."

And he took Peter back to the **boat** where all the other disciples were standing staring at them with their mouths wide open.

Water into Wine

Wedding - Mime holding a camera and say "Click!"
Wine - Make popping sound with finger in mouth
Whispered/Whisper - Put hand to mouth and make whispering sounds:"Psst pssst pssst!"
Servants - Stand and bow
Water - "Splash!"
Nodded - Nod vigorously

One day Jesus's mum was invited to a **wedding** in a place called Cana. As she was getting ready to go she said to Jesus, "Why don't you come too, and you can bring your friends if you like, I'm sure they won't mind."

So they all went along and things were going really well. Then - disaster struck! The **wine** ran out, there had been more guests than expected and they had drunk all the **wine.** Jesus's mum took him to one side and **whispered** in his ear.

"Jesus, why don't you do something, I'm sure you could help sort out the problem before everyone finds out what's happened."

Jesus thought about this for a minute then said, "I'm not sure mother, remember I must do what my father says, not just what my mother says. This may not be the time for me to do a miracle."

Mary **nodded** but then she went ahead and told the **servants** at the **wedding** to do whatever Jesus told them to do.

Jesus looked about and spotted six large stone **water** jars standing in a line along a wall. He beckoned to a **servant** and called him over.

"See those **water** jars," he said. "How much do they hold?"

"An awful lot," said the **servant,** "about twenty five gallons each."

Jesus smiled and **nodded.** "Fill them all up with **water,"** he said.

The **servant nodded** and did as he was told, other **servants** came to help him. When they had done this Jesus beckoned to the servant again.

"Scoop out some of the **water** and take it to the master in charge of today's festivities."

The **servant** raised an eyebrow, then **nodded** and scooped out some **water.** He took it over to the master and braced himself as the master tasted the **water.** There was a moment of silence and the **servant** got ready to run, then suddenly the master slapped him on the back.

"This is wonderful stuff!" he said. "I must congratulate the bridegroom on saving the very best **wine** till last. Dish it out to all the guests."

Jesus's friends were amazed, the **water** had really turned into **wine** and there was more than enough for everyone at the **wedding.** Not many of them knew how it had happened though, Jesus didn't shout about the miracle, he didn't even **whisper** about it, he kept it quiet. Only a few people knew about the amazing thing that had happened.

The Sermon

Humble - Mime applauding the person next to you
Gentle - Mime picking up a little bird, watch it fly off
Kind - Pat someone else on the back
Peaceful - Sigh and relax
Clean - Brush dust off hands
Salt/y - Lick finger and taste and nod

One day, as a large crowd of people gathered around Jesus, he took his closest friends up onto a hill top and began to preach them a sermon.

He said: "It's best to be **humble,** not proud. Then you'll be much happier. It's better to be **gentle** and small than big and confident. It's better to be **kind** and caring to people, for then other people will be kind and caring to you. It's a good idea to try and be **peaceful**, not aggressive, and even if people aren't nice to you it's worth it to you to try and be good, so try and be the best you can for God. Try and keep your hearts and minds **clean** and pure, and always fight for **justice** and truth. And if people get angry and upset with you because you follow me, don't worry, that's good news, because up in heaven God has a brilliant reward for you. He likes you doing these things, even if other people don't.

If you do all these things, be **humble,** be **gentle,** be **kind,** be **peaceful,** be **clean,** then you will be happy - because God will make you happy. And this will make you like **salt** which makes things taste good, you will make the world taste good, because you will be different to other people, and other people will notice. It'll be like standing on a hill under a spotlight, no one will be able to miss it. It'll be dazzling. So be **salty** and let the world taste the difference that God can make."

Going Through the Roof

Roof - "Oooh! ahhh!"
Friends - Thumbs up
Tiles - "Smash!"
Faith - Put hands together and squeeze tight
Sins - A sharp intake of breath - "Haa!" and look shocked
Walk - Stamp feet twice

One day Jesus was telling stories to some folks in a house. It was a very nice house with beautiful paintwork and nice furniture and good floors. Oh and the **roof** was a work of art. Well, while Jesus was talking some **friends** of mine came over to me and said, "Hey, let's take you to see Jesus, he's good with legs."

You see, I hadn't walked for a good few years and my **friends** had heard the Jesus could fix people like me. So before I could argue they picked me up and taxied me over to this beautiful house. Well, there was so many people that it was impossible for them to get in. So I said, "Oh well, never mind, maybe next time." So then one of my **friends** says, "The **roof.**" And I said, "The **roof?**" And they all nodded and said, "The **roof!**" And before you could say elevator they'd dragged me up the side of this house and out onto the roof. Well there was no way in so they started ripping the **tiles** off and making a right mess. It was such a beautiful **roof** too. Such craftsmanship and there they were throwing the bits about as if it was confetti at a wedding. Next thing you know they pick me up and throw me through the hole they've made! Well, maybe not throw, they lowered me down, but I didn't know what was going on. There was dust and dirt and bits of **tiles** everywhere, all over the paintwork and the floors. Heart-breaking!

Anyway, next thing you know there's a bump and a crash and there I am lying on the floor and looking up at the man himself, Jesus. Well you know how tongue-tied you get when you meet the Queen? Well this was the King - of the entire universe. I didn't know what to say, so I just said, "Er ab, well, mm, er, mmm, ab, eh oh!"

But it didn't matter because Jesus wasn't looking at me, he was looking up, at all the damage! Oh dear I thought, we're in a mess now.

Then he said, "I can see your friends have got a lot of **faith."**

I could see it too, making all that mess and expecting to get away with it! A lot of **faith!** But Jesus didn't mean that. He was talking about all the trouble they'd gone to, then he looked at me and said, "My friend, your **sins** are forgiven!" Which was good news and bad news, because I wanted to know how he knew about all my **sins!** My **friends** were surprised too, they'd wanted me to walk, not be forgiven.

But then Jesus smiled and said, "I know what you're thinking, only God can forgive **sins,** well, I'll prove it to you. Which is easier to say, your **sins** are forgiven, or get up and **walk?"**

No one said anything, so he said, "I'll prove that I can say both, my friend, get up and **walk."** And he offered me his hand.

Guess what happened? Well, I didn't **walk** home... I ran! And I hopped and I skipped and I turned cartwheels, all the way home and then round the town afterwards. Jesus fixed my legs and I can **walk** again. Brilliant!

116

A Woman with a Lot of Faith

Please - Hold up hands clasped and pleading   **No** - Hand up, refusing
Food - Mime eating your favourite food
Children - All the children cheer   **Daughter** - All the girls cheer

I want to tell you a story to encourage you to keep on talking to Jesus - even if you don't seem to be getting through. I once have a **daughter**. One day she got very ill and I tried everything to help make her better, but nothing worked. Then one day we heard about Jesus. Everyone said he was a miracle worker, a man of God, a prophet who could do anything, that's what everyone said. He could solve any problem, so maybe, just maybe, he could help me and my **daughter**. We lived up in the hills and when I heard that Jesus was coming to the towns below I got ready and went down to find him.

Well, he wasn't difficult to spot, he was surrounded by people talking and shouting. I did my best to get through the crowd but there was too many of them. So I grabbed one of his friends, Simon I think he was called, and I said to him,

"**Please** tell Jesus I want to see him. I need him to help my **daughter**."

But Simon said, "**No**, go away."

The cheek of it! So I tried again.

"**Please**, just tell him I need to see him."

"**No**!" says Simon.

"**Please**!" I said.

"**No**!

"**Please**!"

"**No**!"

"**Please**!"

"**No**!"

"**Please**!"

"**No**!"

"Please, please, please, pleeeeeeeeeeeease..."

And I went on and on and on and on and on and on and on and on and on and on and on...

Suddenly there was Jesus, standing next to Simon.

"Will you do something about this woman?" he said. "She's driving me crackers!"

And you know what? Jesus looked at me and said, "**No**."

I couldn't believe it.   "**No**!" he said "**No**!"

"Why not?"   I said. "You can do anything. Everyone says so."

"I've got to help these people here," said Jesus. "I'm busy right now."

And you know what I said? I fell on my knees and said,

"**Pleeeeeeeeeeeeeeeeeeeeeeeeeeeeeeeeeeeeeeeease!**"

Well poor old Jesus looked a bit shocked.

"It isn't right to help you now," he said. "There are so many needy people here, they're just like **children**. It would be like taking **food** out of a child's mouth if I helped you."

"Ah," I said, "but sometimes **children** don't always finish up their **food**, they have leftovers. So can't you just give me some of the leftovers?"

Jesus looked at me and laughed.

"You're very astute," he said, "and you have a lot of faith. How can I refuse? Your prayer is answered now go home!"

And when I got back what d'you think I found? My **daughter** alive and well, and wanting to know why tea wasn't ready yet!

Who is Jesus?

Person - Pat the person next to you on the back or shoulder
Answer - snap fingers   **Teacher** - Sit up straight
Hero - strike heroic pose   **Doctor** - Hold elbow as if it hurts
Prophet - Put hand to ear and listen
Friend - Shake hands with person next to you

One day Jesus gathered his friends round him and said to them, "Who d'you think I am?"

"Don't you know?" they said.

"Of course I know," said Jesus, "but I'm not sure if you do."

"Oh I do," said Andrew, "it's obvious, everybody says you're a really good **person**. You're a great example to follow."

"No, that's not the **answer**," said Matthew "you're a really good **teacher**, you tell brilliant stories too."

"No," said James, "I reckon you're a **hero**, you're gonna conquer the world."

"No," said Phillip, "you're a really good **doctor**. You've cured loads of people, even some dead ones."

"No," said Thomas, "you're a really good **prophet**. You tell us all about God."

"No," said John, "you're a really good **friend**. You really care about people and they can rely on you."

"No," said Peter, and suddenly everyone else fell silent.

"You're more than all of those," he said. "It's true that you're a good **person**, **teacher**, **hero**, **doctor**, **prophet** and **friend**, but you're also different to anyone who's ever lived before. You're the Son of God."

Jesus smiled and said, "Well done Peter."

And all the others wished they'd thought of that **answer**, but they hadn't, because it wasn't just a good idea, it was something that God had told to Peter so that you and might know it too.

The Unforgiving Cook

Big - Hold out hands to show a large size
Eggs - "Crack!"
Supermarket - "Beep Beep!"
Pay - Pat pockets as if looking for money
Party - All cheer
Barry the Boss - Salute and bow

Once there was a cook called Cheerful Charlie, who worked for a rich man called **Barry the Boss**. One day Charlie decided to lay on a **party** for all his friends. So he went out and bought all the best food, caviar, haggis, champagne and lots of sticky toffee pudding. He bought twice as much as he needed, and he had a lot of friends so the bill was quite **big**. Too **big** for his own credit card. So when he came to **pay** he told the supermarket to put it on his boss's bill. As he pushed the trolley out to his car he bumped into one of his friends, Kev the Chef.

"Lend me a couple of **eggs**," pleaded Kev, "you've got loads there and I want to make an omelette for my tea." Charlie took a couple of **eggs** out of his basket and gave them to Kev the chef.

A week later Charlie had his **party** and all his friends were there, eating and drinking and having a good time. Suddenly the doors burst open and everywhere fell silent as Barry the Boss stormed in.

"What's all this?" he yelled and he held up a very long bill from the supermarket. "Have you seen how **big** this bill is?"

Charlie didn't look cheerful at that moment. He looked very scared.

"I spent too much on the **party** and I can't **pay** you back." he whimpered.

Barry the Boss took a slow, careful look round the room. Then he sighed, shook his head... and smiled.

"That's okay," he said. "Have the **party** on me."

So they did.

Ten minutes later Charlie spotted Kev the Chef jigging away on the dance floor.

"Hey!" yelled Charlie, "you owe me two **eggs**!"

"Oh dear," said Kev, "I haven't got any **eggs** on me right now."

"In that   case," said Charlie, "I'm gonna triple it to six. You owe me six **eggs** now, and I won't forget it! Ever!"

Just then Charlie felt a hand grab him warmly by the throat.

"Uggghhh!" said Charlie.

It was **Barry the Boss**.

"Oh oh," said Kev, "I think you're in **big** trouble."

"He certainly is," said **Barry the Boss**, "I let him off a very **big** bill, and he couldn't let you have two **eggs** for an omelette. You're in **very** big trouble Cheerful Charlie!"

The Poor Rich Man

Rich - Throw notes in the air and shout "Flutter, flutter, flutter"
Suits - Brush shoulders and look proud
Ties - Straighten tie
Coats - Mime buttoning up coat
Hats - Pull on a hat
Heaven - Scratch head and look puzzled

There was once a very, very, very, very... nice man. Who was also very **rich**.

He had two hundred posh **suits**, a hundred posh **ties**, fifty posh **coats** and twenty posh **hats**. He had everything. Everything. But, he felt as if there was something missing and he wasn't sure what it might be.

So when he heard that Jesus was coming to town he decided he'd better go and see him.

So he opened his wardrobe and picked out his poshest **suit**, poshest **tie**, poshest **hat** and poshest **coat** and then he went into town to see Jesus. On the way he wondered what he could say to Jesus to start up a conversation, and he decided to ask him about **heaven**.

In the town Jesus was walking and talking with his friends when the **rich** man arrived. He smiled when he saw the man and gave him a big wave.

"Hello," said the **rich** man, "I've come to ask you a question. How do I get to **heaven**?"

"Well," said Jesus, "it's very important to listen to God and to do the things he says."

"What sort of things?"

"Always tell the truth, try and treat other people the way you would like to be treated, don't steal things, don't hurt things, and definitely don't kill anything."

"I do all that," said the **rich** man, "but there's still something missing."

Jesus stopped and thought for a while.

"Yes," he said. "I think you're right. How many **suits** have you got? How many **ties**? How many **coats**? How many **hats**?"

The **rich** man told him.

"How long would it take you to give them all away?" Jesus asked.

"A very long time," said the **rich** man, "because I don't want to give them all away."

"Then that's the answer," said Jesus, "you've got so many other things in your life that you haven't got much room for God. Give away all those **suits**, **ties**, **coats** and **hats** and then you'll be happy."

The **rich** man shook his head and turned and walked slowly away, he felt very mixed up because he really loved all his nice clothes, yet deep down he wondered if Jesus might be right.

123

A Flat Fee

Foundation - Stamp feet twice - "Stamp! Stamp!"
£200 - "Whooo!" and look impressed
Contract - "Scribble scribble"
Any kind of food - Make eating noises
Mistake - Sharp intake of breath and put hand to mouth

Once there was a man who decided to build his own house. He knew nothing about building houses but he thought it couldn't be that difficult, so he bought a nice plot of land and started to dig the **foundations**. However, he made a big **mistake**, he built the house very quickly and it didn't last long, because he built it in a day and on a swamp with no **foundations**. Overnight it collapsed and fell on top of him while he was asleep and when he woke up the next morning, the toilet had collapsed, the windows had dropped out, and most of the roof had fallen in his mouth. So he decided to try again, this time he wouldn't make the same **mistake**, this time he bought a bit of land that was good and solid, and this time he decided to get some help.

So he went into the nearby town and found some people sitting around on the bench outside the job centre.
"I want some help to build my house," he said. "I want it done properly with good **foundations** and a nice little fountain in the garden."
But the people said they were too busy having a rest.
So he said, "I'll pay you all **£200** if you'll help me. Plus lots of free **food**."
Suddenly they weren't so busy, and they leapt up, signed a **contract** and started work on the house.
At coffee time he went into town to buy some **doughnuts** for everyone and he spotted some a large group of people on the bench outside the job centre.
"Want to earn a few quid?" he asked them, they all leapt up and he had to buy twice as many **doughnuts**.

At lunchtime the man went into town to buy some **veggie burgers** for lunch. He spotted some more people outside the job centre.

"Want to help me build a house?" he asked them and they got up and helped him carry the **veggie burgers** back to the building site.

At teatime he went in for some **cream cakes** and saw another crowd. So he asked them for help too.

By the time they'd finished work the field was full of workers and empty food bags.

"Come and collect your wages," the man shouted.

The tea time recruits lined up first and the man paid   them each **£200**.

"Excellent!" said the lunch time recruits, "we'll get twice as much."

"Cool!" said the coffee time recruits. "We'll get three times as much!"

"Even better," said the morning recruits, "we'll get four times as much."

But they didn't, they all got **£200**. There was nearly a riot.

"That's not fair," they said. "We've worked all day and only got the same as the people who just did a bit at the end."

"Oh dear," said the man, "I must have made a **mistake**."

So the man took out their **contracts** and had a look.

"No, that's right," he said. "Look, you agreed to work all day for **£200**. It says so here."

"Yes, but..."

 "No, buts," said the man. "There's no **mistake**. It's my money, if I want to be generous that's up to me. There's no need for you to get stingy about it."

The Pharisee and Tax Collector

Divide the congregation into two, side one must play the part of the first person, the other side the second person. The format is simple, no lines or responses to learn here, each side must simply repeat their lines of dialogue as they hear them. So, when those on side one hear the line:
The first one went inside and said confidently "Hello Lord it's me again!"
they must repeat this dialogue confidently. When those on the second side hear their cue to say this, they must repeat it sadly.
You may like to choose two people to come out and lead each side as they repeat their lines.
The message of the story in this case is not in the words, it is in the manner of speech. I have chosen this style as it reflects the message of the sketch, that it is not whether or not we pray, it is how we pray, both men went to the temple to talk to God, but only one was forgiven.

There were once two people who went to church to pray.
The first one went inside and said confidently:
"Hello Lord, it's me again!"
The second one went inside and said sadly: "Hello Lord, it's me again."
The first one said loudly, "I bet you remember me Lord!"
The second one said quietly, "I bet you remember me Lord."
The first one looked up and said, "Look at him over there."
The second one looked down and said, "Look at him over there."
The first one said, "Lord, you know I am not like him."
The second one said, "Lord, you know I am not like him."
The first one nodded and said, "I have done so many things."
The second one shook his head and said, "I have done so many things."
Then together they said, "Thank you Lord for your love and forgiveness."

Then they got up and left.
The first person went away proud and happy.
But the second person went away humble and forgiven.

The Three Thieves

Thief/thieves - Scowl and look menacing
Tiptoed - Mime tiptoeing
Head - Pull mask on
Karate - Take up a karate stance
Shotgun - Hold rifle

Once there were three people living in three houses full of wonderful things. And there were three **thieves** who were planning to break into these three houses and steal all the wonderful things. The first **thief** waited until eight o'clock pulled a balaclava over his **head** and **tiptoed** down the garden path of house number one. He found an open window and slipped it up. Then he crept inside and got a shock, because the owner, a sweet old lady called Mrs A Lert, was sitting inside with a **shotgun,** two Rottweilers and a stick of dynamite, and the moment he broke in she called the police and held him at **gun** point until they
arrived.

The second **thief** waited until nine o'clock, then he pulled a gorilla mask on his **head, tiptoed** up the garden path to house number two. He slipped open the kitchen window, climbed inside and also got a shock. The owner, a gentle ex-nun called Miss V. Sharp, had been taking **karate** lessons and as soon as the **thief** landed in her kitchen sink, she put him in an arm lock, flung him over her shoulder, swung him round by the neck, tied his feet around his elbows and knocked him out with a karate chop. When he woke up he was in a police cell with back ache, head ache, leg ache and bottom ache.

The third **thief** wrapped a scarf around his **head, tiptoed** up the garden path, then tripped up on his way as he couldn't see a thing. He tried to prize open a window but broke his crowbar as he was doing it. So he smashed a very big and loud hole in the front door and walked in through it. Inside he helped himself to the television, the DVD player, the surround-sound system, the CD collection, the complete works of Shakespeare and the fridge.

He carried them all outside in one big pile and put his back out on the way. Then he loaded up his van, and drove off, accidentally knocking the greenhouse down as he drove through it.

But in spite of all his bungling, the third **thief** got away with a fortune, because the owner of the house, a Mr Neveready, had sent his guard dog to the vet, his **shotgun** to the menders, his telephone was disconnected because he'd not paid the bills and he'd taken up origami instead of **karate** lessons.

So when the **thief** came, Mr Neveready, was never ready.

In the same way God may drop by and visit us anytime, and like Miss V. Sharp and Mrs A. Lert, we should always be on the look out and ready for anything.

Creation's Ovations

Look - Point into the distance
Run - Run on the spot, sitting or standing
Coat - Zip up a coat   **Salute** - Salute
Anger/Angry – Snarl   **Sun/Sunny** - Wipe sweat from brow
Shout - Open mouth wide and place hands to open mouth
Dance/Jitter/Jive/Roll/Creole - Jive in your seats
Sneeze - Make a sneezing noise

A dust road - Palm trees - A bright **sunny** day
Disciples on a long walk - They followed the way.
They came down to a town - The people did say:
"**Look** now - Jesus is coming today!"

Panic - Scramble - Pick up your **coat**
Run run - Down the road - Don't miss the boat.
Look look - The Son of God - He's coming ya know
Everybody's getting down - Don't you be slow.

Throw down - Your **coats** now - Down on the side
Branches - Rip 'em off and pile 'em up high.
The Son of God - **Salute** him - "Hosanna!" they cry
Palm leaves and **coat** sleeves - Stick 'em up high.

The Pharisees weren't pleased - **Anger** abounds!
"Palm leaves - **Coat** sleeves - Put 'em down!"
They said: "Stop that - Cut the noise - Keep it down!"
"Or there will be a lot of **angry** people around."

Jesus - Got 'em sussed - He don't care
Even if they lock up all the people there,
The **salutes** and the praise would still go out -
The rocks and the trees - They'd all just **shout.**

The stones and the dust would **shout** out too:
"Look out everybody - Here's the saviour for you!"
Creation's Ovations would carry the news,
The trees would **sneeze:** "He's the King of the Jews."

The plants would **dance** and the rocks would **roll;**
The **sun** would shine and the clouds **creole;**
The litter would **jitter** and the rubbish **jive;**
Everything agrees that He's alive!

So join the song - Come on - **Shout** along!
Rejoice with your voice and make it strong.
Dance in the dust and leap in the light -
For Jesus just visited your town tonight...

The Parable of the Talents

Use counting - holding up fingers
Ask everyone to raise the correct number of fingers whenever they hear a numerical word - including those which sound numerical - *to* and *for*. This is a technique which could be applied to many Bible stories, particularly those which have some kind of numerical content.

There was once a man of high rank who was going to a country far away to be made king. After which he planned to come back. One day, before he left, he called his ten servants and gave them each one gold coin and told them, "See what you can earn with this while I am gone."
The man was made king and came back. At once he ordered his ten servants to appear before him, in order to find out what they had earned. The first one came in and said, "Sir, I have earned ten gold coins with the one you gave me."
"Well done," he said, "since you were faithful in small matters I will put you in charge of ten cities."
The second servant came and said, "Sir, I have earned five gold coins with the one you gave me."
To this one he said, "You will be in charge of five cities."

A third servant came in and said, "Sir, here is your one gold coin; I kept it hidden in a handkerchief. I was afraid of you, for you are a hard man. You take what is not yours and reap what you did not sow."
He said to him, "You bad servant! I will use your own words to condemn you! You know that I am a hard man. Well, then, why didn't you put my money in the bank? Then I would have received it back with five or six % interest when I returned."
Then he said to those who were standing there, "Take the one gold coin away from him and give it to the servant who has ten coins." But they said to him, "Sir, he already has ten coins - that'll make eleven!" "I tell you," he replied, "that to every person who has something, more will be given..."

Easter

Fireworks - *Fizz bang!*
Turkey - *Eat drumstick*
Parties - *"Cheers"*
Cards - *"Kiss, kiss, kiss"*
Flowers - *Sniff them and sneeze*
Chocolate - *"Mmmmm!"*

On Guy Fawkes Night we have **fireworks**.
At Christmas we have **turkey**.
At New Year we have **parties**.
On Valentine's Day we have **cards**.
For Mother's day we have **flowers**.
So what do we have for Easter?
Chocolate!

Fireworks light up the night.
Turkey seems to last for ever.
Parties can be wild.
Cards talk about love.
Flowers have to die.
And all of those things can remind us of Easter.

Like the **fireworks** - Easter is about lighting up the darkness.
Like the **turkey** - it'll last forever.
Like the **parties** - it's wild and can't be contained.
Like the **cards** - it's all about love.
And like the **flowers** have to die - at Easter we remember a man who had
to die.

At Easter we give **chocolate** eggs - but the first Easter present came from
above -
It was the gift of a man called Jesus, who came to earth like a bright
vibrant **firework**, to bring us a message of love.

Peter and John Heal a Man

Part one:
Three o'clock - "Bong, bong, bong!"
Footsteps - Make sound of steps with hands or feet
Flapped/Fluttered - Make fluttering, flapping sounds
Part two:
Divide the audience/congregation into two.
One side echoes the words of the two men. The other side echo the words of the lame man.
You will need two people to lead these echoed responses, as it is not always clear from the text which side is speaking.

It was almost **three o'clock** in the afternoon. The city was deserted. No one around. Down through the centre of town the sound of **footsteps** came echoing. The **footsteps**... grew louder and louder, and faster and faster. Somewhere in the distance a bird flapped its wings and fluttered away. More **footsteps**. Who was coming to town on that quiet afternoon? The seconds ticked by, and suddenly... it was **three o'clock**.
Two men stepped into the town square, they paused, looked around and then made for temple. They reached the door, their **footsteps** faltered, then from nowhere a voice called out,
"**Got any loose change?**"

The men stopped dead and looked down. Just beside the town gateway there was a lame man, sitting begging.
"**We're broke,**" said the men, "**we haven't even got a penny on us.**"
"**Can't you spare anything at all?**" asked the man.
The men looked at one another, then they smiled.
"**We don't have any money but we can give you something else.**"
They held out their hands. The lame mane craned his neck to see what they were holding.
"**Come on. Reach out and take it,**" they said.
"**But there's nothing there,**" said the lame man, and he put out his hand as he said this.

They grabbed him and hauled him to his feet.

"**We don't have money,**" they said, "**but we have faith. In the name of Jesus of Nazareth, get up and walk!**"

And before he knew what had happened the lame man was up and on his feet and his legs were suddenly strong and full of pins and needles and he started to run about and leap in the air and dance and shout.

"**I can walk! I can walk!**" he said.

The men carried on walking into the temple.

"**Where are you going? Can I come too?**" asked the man, and without waiting for a reply he followed them inside.

Everything in the temple was quiet and peaceful... until the lame man walked in and everyone recognised him and saw the miracle, then there was chaos and everyone was amazed.

The City of Light

Drop - Hold one hand out flat and drop other hand onto it with a loud clap
City - Half say: "Beep! Beep!" Other half say: "Mind the gap!"
People - Point towards someone else   **Lion/s** - All roar
Dream/s - Look amazed, say "Wow!"   **Snakes** - All hiss and wriggle

Once there was a man called John, he lived on an island and one day, on a Sunday, he was praying quietly on his own when suddenly he saw an amazing thing. It was like an amazing technicolour **dream** complete with surround sound. He saw a huge **city drop** out of the sky in front of him, full of colour and light. It was just like watching a huge spaceship **drop** out of the sky at the cinema on the big screen, only this was bigger and this was real and John could actually get up and walk into the **city**. As he walked about through the bright clean shining streets, he saw lots of **people** who were really happy. Nobody was sad, and nobody was frightened and nobody was angry with anyone else. No one was ill or injured and **people** were living happily together, and their best **dreams** were all coming true, and there was room for everyone to live together in amazing houses.

John turned a corner and saw a **lion** walk towards him, but he needn't have worried, because the **lion** was walking with a lamb, and also with a calf, and there was a bear too and playing with them all was a group of children. And no one got hurt, because all the animals ate grass. Even the **snakes** didn't hurt anyone.

John looked in amazement and wonder at all this and then he realised where he was. This was God's **city**, this was the **city** where God lived and that's why it was a place of safety and protection and peace and life.
And John knew that one day he would live there, one day all God's people would live in those houses and walk along those streets and play with the **lions** and the wild animals. And God would be their next door neighbour.

Then the **city** rose up and disappeared again, and John grabbed some paper and quickly wrote down everything he had seen.

Big J and Rocky

Stick/Stuck - Press shoulder against person nearby, make a sticky noise
Truth - Raise right hand and nod solemnly as if in court giving evidence
Listens - Place hand to ear   **Laugh** - All laugh loudly
Good and bad times - Smile then look sad
Happy and sad times - As above, smile then look sad
Cry - All cry loudly   **Eat/Ate** - Make loud eating sounds

Now hopefully we all have a friend or two.

A friend is someone who **sticks** by you.

A friend tells you the **truth**.

A friend **listens** to you.

A friend is there for the **good and bad times**.

For the **happy and sad times**.

Once there were two friends who promised to always **stick** by each other. They went everywhere together. They **ate** meals together, they **laughed, listened** and **cried** together. They were called Big J and Rocky. And they were the best of friends. Then one day things went wrong. Big J got arrested for something he didn't do, in short he was framed. And though Rocky had promised to always **stick** by him, he didn't - he got scared and ran away. Poor Big J was left all on his own. After a while Rocky did try and help, he went along to the police station and waited outside, but then someone recognised him and said, "You're Big J's friend." But Rocky pretended to **laugh** and said, "No, not me." He broke the second rule of friends then, he didn't tell the **truth.** He was just very scared.

Well a few days went by and Rocky didn't see Big J again. He felt really **bad** and feared that they might never be friends again. But then, one morning, while Rocky was out fishing on the beach, Rocky was a very good fisherman, by the way, suddenly he saw Big J standing there.

Well Rocky just stared, he didn't know what to do, after all, he'd not **stuck** by Big J, he'd not told the **truth,** and he'd not been there in the **bad** times and the **sad times**. But then Big J smiled and **laughed** and said, "Hey why don't we **eat** some breakfast together, I'm starving."

So Rocky stood up ran over to Big J and gave him a big hug. And while they **ate** breakfast Rocky discovered the most important thing about friendship, because Big J forgave him for letting him down and running away. And the two were best friends once again.

The Truth Twins

Dazzbone LeShuttle - "Sssssss! Boooo!"   **Days** - Eyes wide look alert
Nights - Shut eyes and shore   **Truth** - Place open hand in front of you
Lies – hold out hand and pull away into a fist (i.e. hiding the truth away)
Chased/Chasing - Pant   **Jail** - "Clang!"   **Nope** - All shake heads
Bridge - Make a creaking noise   **Yep** - All nod vigorously

One day, Walter Crashtest, a famous private investigator, was trying to track down his arch enemy **Dazzbone LeShuttle**. He **chased** him for **days** and **nights** and **nights** and **days**, over mountains and through canyons and under the sea. **Dazzbone LeShuttle** was a very dangerous criminal and a threat to the safety of mankind, so Walter Crashtest had to keep **chasing** him until he could catch him and lock him up forever in Moonstone **Jail**. He had just begun to catch up with **Dazzbone** when he came to a rickety rope **bridge** over a huge yawning chasm. The chasm was way too wide to cross, except over the **bridge**, but Walter wasn't sure if it would take his weight. He looked over and saw that far down, in the canyon below, the white water was foaming and fat grey alligators sat on the rocky banks waiting for something to eat. He was wondering what to do when suddenly up popped a pair of identical twins.

"Hello," they said, "we're the **truth** twins. We're the keepers of the rickety **bridge**."

"Is it strong enough for me to cross?" asked Walter. "Only I'm chasing **Dazzbone LeShuttle**, my arch enemy and I much catch him and lock him up in Moonstone **Jail**. I've been chasing him for **days** and **nights.** But I'm heavier than he is, and I might bring the **bridge** down."

"Before we answer we must warn you," said the **truth** twins, "one of us always tells the   **truth**   and the other one of us always tells **lies**."

"What?" said Walter. "One of you always tell the **truth** and the other one always tells **lies**?"

"**Yep**," they said, "one of us always tell the **truth** and the other one always tells **lies**."

"Oh, so you," Walter pointed to the tallest one, "will the **bridge** hold me?"

"**Yep**," said the twin. "Sure will."

"And you," Walter pointed to the shortest one, "will the **bridge** hold me."

"**Nope**," said the twin. "Sure won't."

"Oh," said Walter, "this is ridiculous. I don't know who to believe. Didn't anyone ever tell you - you should always speak the **truth**."

"**Yep**," said the tallest. "**Nope**," said the shortest.

"Didn't you know that **lies** can cause big trouble for people?"

"**Yep**," said the tallest. "**Nope**," said the shortest.

Walter paced up and down. Who should he believe? The tallest said the **bridge** was okay. The shortest said it wasn't. He looked form one twin to the other, then he looked back at the rickety **bridge**. Then he snapped his fingers.

"I've got it," he said.

"Have you?" said the twins.

"Yes!" he turned to the tallest one. "If I asked him, the short one, what would he say? You tell me."

There was silence. Walter knew that whatever answer the twin gave would include a **lie**.

"He would say," said the twin, "he would say... the **bridge** won't hold you."

Walter snapped his fingers again.

"Bingo!" he said. "Then it will hold me."

And without another word he leaped on the rope **bridge** ran across safe and sound and ambushed **Dazzbone LeShuttle** as he was sleeping in the trees on the other side. Then he took him back and locked him up in Moonstone **Jail**.

Little Dog Moffet Finds the Sun

Any colour - All point to that colour if you can see it anywhere
Sun - Hold up hand in sky as if it is the sun and waggle it
Time - "Tick tick tick tick...."
Journey/ed - "Chug chug chug chug..."
Chin - Rub your chin

Little Dog Moffet stood near the edge of Tungsten Cliff and watched the
orange sun drop down behind the **blue** sea.
"There must be a hundred of those over there," he said to himself.
"Because one drops down there every night after tea."
Little Dog Moffet decided right there and then he would go to the edge of
time and take a look.
He would sail across the sea to where the **sun** dropped down, no matter
how long the **journey** took.

Little Dog Moffet went straight home, packed his bags and picked up his
phone,
He called up his best friend, told him the plan and asked, "Will you come
with me, if you can?"
His friend was called Ragged Bone and they had been best friends for
years.
Little Dog Moffet had big **brown** eyes, a double **chin** and huge floppy
ears.
Ragged Bone was smaller than Little Dog, and he only had a single **chin**.
But he was just as brave and if Little Dog wanted to find the **sun**, then
Ragged Bone would go with him.

They set sail in a boat made out of an upside-down car.
They filled it with food and water and dog biscuits by the jar
They sailed for days and nights and **journeyed** long beneath the **sun**.
And eventually they reached the edge of **time** and this is what they came
upon.

They found a place full of **golden** light,
Where the **sun** drops down and disappears every night.
And there they found an angel all dressed in **white**.
And when he saw them he smiled and said, "How ya   doing, all right?"

He gave them a drink and they sat on little **blue** seats and had a chat.
"We've come to find the **sun**," said Little Dog, and Ragged Bone said,
"Amen to that!"
"It's not here," said the angel. "it never stops moving, it goes on all night.
It's gone to Australia and New Zealand with its **orange** warmth and light."
"Where's it come from? And how did it start?" asked Ragged Bone.
"It started a long long time ago," said the angel, "when the Creator was
here all on his own.
He had a bright idea and he made the **sun**.
Then he got carried away and made people and birds and animals and fish
and **green** grass and **brown** trees and **blue** lakes and **red** worms and
yellow and **black** bees and **purple** sharks and **stripy** sabre-toothed tigers
and **grey** woolly mammoths... and he had an awful lot of fun."
Then Little Dog Moffet and Ragged Bone said goodbye to the angel and
set sail for home.
As they sat in the boat and watched the stars and the beautiful **orange sun**,
They thought about the Creator and of how it had all begun.

Treat Everyone the Same

Nice – Smile   **Nasty** - Growl
Big - Look up   **Little** - Look down
Rich - Rub fingers together
Poor - Look at empty hands
Busy - Wipe brow and sigh loudly
Lazy - Yawn and lean back   **At work** - Type furiously
On holiday - Slap sun cream on face, say "Slap, slap!" for each cheek
Quiet - "Shhhh!"   **Noisy** - Shout "Oi!"
Friendly - Smile and wave
Not so friendly - Shake fist and snarl

It's a good idea to treat everyone the same. When it's a hot day the sun shines on everyone doesn't it? It shines on the **nice** people and the **nasty** people, it shines on the **rich** people and the **poor** people. It shines on the **big** people and the **little** people, it shines on the **busy** people and the **lazy** people. It shines on the people at **work** and the people on **holiday.** Whether they're **quiet** or **noisy**, **friendly** or **not so friendly**. When it rains and we need the water, it rains on the **nice** people and the **nasty** people, it rains on the **rich** people and the **poor** people. It rains on the **big** people and the **little** people, it rains on the **busy** people and the **lazy** people. It rains on the people at **work** and the people on **holiday.** Whether they're **quiet** or **noisy**, **friendly** or **not so friendly**. And when it snows, it snows on the... (*Say this list really fast now*) **nice, nasty, rich, poor, busy, lazy, at work, on holiday**. God sends the same weather on us and treats us the same. So try and treat people the same, whether they're **nice, nasty, big, little, rich, poor, busy, lazy, quiet, noisy, friendly** or **not so friendly**. Try not to judge or criticise just because people are different, remember - to them you look different. So, whether they're **nice, nasty, big, little, rich, poor, busy, lazy, quiet, noisy, friendly** or **not so friendly** - let them bring out the best in you, not the worst.

Houses & Homes

Igloos - Shiver and say "Brrrrr!"
Caravans - Jig up and down in seats as if on a bumpy road
Castles - Shout - "Lower the drawbridge!"
Prisons - "Let me out!"
Farms - Make different animal sounds
Church/es/Temple – (sing) "A-a-a-amen."

Some people live in **igloos**. Some live in **caravans**. Some live in **castles**. Some live in **prisons**. Some live in **farms**. Now, who lives in **Igloos**? (Wait for answer) Who lives in **caravans**? (Wait for an answer) Who lives in **castles**? (Wait for an answer) Who lives in **prisons**? (Wait for an answer) Who lives in **farms**? (Wait for an answer)

And then there are **churches**. Now who might live in a **church**?

Now you might think God does - but he doesn't. We think of a **church** as God's house, but he doesn't actually live there. Years and years ago people made a beautiful **temple** for him to live in, it was called Solomon's **temple**. But nowadays it's different, God doesn't want a building, because he can live in me and you. And that's where he wants to settle down and make his home - in us. In our lives and hearts and families. It's a bit like saying we are a **temple** now for God to live in. A **church** is just a place where we can meet together and talk to him and listen to him. After all if God lived in a **church**, when we went home and closed the doors we'd have locked him inside and he wouldn't be able to get out! But if God lives in us then, wherever we go, God goes there with us. And whoever we meet, God meets them with us. So, just as Eskimos live in **igloos** and kings live in **castles**, God needs a home too. But he doesn't live in a **church** or any kind of building - he lives inside people.

Respect!

Family/Families - Bunch together with those round you and
pose for a family photo
Brothers/Sisters - Boys and girls pull faces at each other or cheer
Pets - "Meow, Woof, Hiss, Squeak!"
Sport - Shout out football teams
Respect - Give the person next to you a high five and say (Coolly) "Hey!"

Families are all different, some are big and some are small
You might have **brothers** and **sisters**, or you might have none at all.
Your parents may be married, or they may live apart
You might live with your step dad, or your granny or an aunt.

You might have step**brothers**, or step**sisters** at large
They may be younger and you may be in charge.
You might have some **pets**, a cat or dog, a snake or mouse
And your family may be tidy, or you might have a messy house.

Your **families** might be working, or some of them might not.
You might have a quiet **family**, or you might be a noisy lot.
You might be into **sport**, cricket, snooker, chess, or running.
Or you might like reading or computers... or doing absolutely nothing.

Whatever sort of **family** you live with in your home
You gotta have **respect** - even if they often moan.
Always give **respect** to those who are older than you
And adults - listen up - give **respect** to those kids too.

Little Dog Moffet Gets Worried

Worried - Say "Oh dear" and look worried
Dream - "Wow!"   **Sleepy** - Yawn
Biscuit/s -"Crunch crunch!"   **Sail** - "Splash!"
Friend/s - Give each other five
Sure - "Say Yes!" and punch the air

Little Dog Moffet was **worried**
He'd never been **worried** before
So he went straight over to his **friend**, Ragged Bone,
And he knocked on his big front door.

Ragged Bone was **sleepy**
He'd only just woken up.
"Hello," he said when he opened the door,
"You look **worried**, what's up?"

Little Dog Moffet told Ragged Bone
He'd had a very bad **dream**.
The sky had fallen on everyone's head
And the sea turned to clotted cream.

"It's just a **dream**," said Ragged Bone,
"A **dream** - that's frightened you."
"Yes," said Little Dog Moffet,
"But suppose it all comes true."

Ragged Bone scratched his head
And chewed on a **biscuit** or two.
"I know," he said, "Let's go and see Dougal,
He'll tell us what to do."

So Little Dog Moffet and Ragged Bone
Set **sail** in an upturned car.
They filled it with food and water
And dog **biscuits** by the jar.

Dougal was a wise old dog
He'd been around a long, long **time.**
He had very long hair and he lived in a house
Right at the edge of **time.**

"I see your problem," said Dougal.
When Ragged Bone told him the score.
"There are many things you can **worry** about
But of one thing you can be **sure**."

"We all have a **friend** in heaven above
And he knows a thing or two.
You can leave your problems and **worries** with him
And he'll help you to know what to do."

So they said a prayer and said goodbye
And then they set **sail** for home.
And Little Dog Moffet now had two **friends.**
One in heaven, and of course, Ragged Bone.

Telling *Even More* Tales

INDEX

Other Stories

Creation

Chaos – Shout "Ahh!" and pull at your ears and hair
Order – All adopt very big smiles indeed
Fingers – Snap fingers
Breath – Breath in deeply and noisily
Hmmm... – Scratch head
Wow! – Punch the air and shout "Wow!"
Empty – Look all around: up, down, in front, behind

In the beginning, way, way back at the dawn of time... there was **chaos**.
And God looked down on the **chaos** and thought "**Hmmm**... time we had some **order**."
So he took a deep **breath**, snapped his **fingers** and turned the **chaos** into **order**.
Then he looked down on the **order** and thought "**Hmmm** it's a bit dark... time we had some light."
So he took a deep **breath**, snapped his **fingers** and turned the darkness into light.
Then he looked down on the light and saw there was lots of water, and he thought "**Hmmm** it's a bit **empty**... time we had some sky."
So he took a deep **breath**, snapped his **fingers** and turned some of the light into sky.

Then he looked down on the water and thought "**Hmmm** it's a bit wet... time we had some dry land."
So he took a deep **breath**, snapped his **fingers** and turned some of the water into dry land.
Then he looked down on the land and thought "**Hmmm** it's a bit **empty**... time we had some trees."
So he took a deep **breath**, snapped his **fingers** and turned the land into forests.

Then he looked down on the forests and thought "**Hmmm** it's a bit **empty**... time we had some animals."
So he took a deep **breath**, snapped his **fingers** and filled the forests with animals.

"**Wow**!" he said, "they're good!" So he filled the sea with fish too and the sky with birds.

Then he looked down on the animals, fish and birds and thought "**Hmmm**... time we had some humans."

So he took a very, very, very deep **breath**, snapped his **fingers**, grabbed a handful of mud, swished it around, blew on it and said, "**Wow**! That's even better."

And there standing on the earth, right in the middle of the forest, right in the middle of the animals, was a man.

And God said, "**Hmmm**... he's a bit lonely... time we made another one of those."

So he took a very, very, very, very, very deep **breath**... snapped his **fingers** and made the man fall asleep. Then he ripped out one of his ribs and used it to make a woman.

"**Wow**!" said God, "now that finishes it off perfectly."

And God sat back, took a rest and said, "Now that's what I call creation."

What's In A Name?

Methuselah – Scratch head, puzzled
Johnny English – Hold hands in karate position
Wallace & Gromit – Say "Cracking Toast Gromit!"
Horrible – "Ugh!"
Worse – "Haaaa!" Shocked
Special – Hold up finger and say "Ding!"
Name – Each person call out own name
Hammer/Saw/Chisel – Divide audience into three, some hammer,
some saw, some chisel
Noise – All hammer, chisel and saw together
Friends – Pat person next to you on the back or arm

Once upon a time there was a man called **Methuselah**. Now **Methuselah** is an unusual **name**. It has a very **special** meaning. It means: when he is dead it shall be sent. **Methuselah**. Strange, isn't it?

Now, **Methuselah** lived in the days of the Old Testament, way, way back in the early days of the Bible. His dad was called Enoch and Enoch was on very good terms with God, in fact you could say they were the best of **friends**.

Well, when **Methuselah** was a little boy a lot of people must have wondered about his **name**. **Methuselah**, they would say, that's a funny **name**! And **Methuselah** might have said, "Well it could be worse, it could be **Johnny English**, or **Wallace & Gromit**…"

But it wasn't **Johnny English**, or **Wallace & Gromit**.

When **Methuselah** grew up he got married and had a little boy of his own called Lamech. In those days people weren't very nice, in fact they were **horrible**, and as the years went by they got **worse**, and **worse**, and **worse**. **Methuselah** and his son were very good **friends** with God, but not many other people were, so up in heaven God began to think of a plan.

Just then, Lamech grew up, got married and had a son of his own. By now, grandfather **Methuselah** was getting quite old, in fact he was 369. Is anybody here today 369? Perhaps a few of us feel it.

Well, the years rolled by, and the people were still **horrible**, and things were still getting **worse**, and **worse**, and **worse**. Until finally, one day God said, enough is enough. I love all the people I've made but this can't go on getting **worse**. I need to find a good carpenter.

Lamech's son was a good carpenter and so God gave him a special job to do, and he set to work **hammering**, **sawing** and **chiselling** and generally making an awful lot of **noise**. And when he'd finished **hammering**, **sawing** and **chiselling** - bingo! He'd made a boat!

His old grandfather **Methuselah**, came to see it and was very proud of his grandson. It was **Methuselah's** birthday and he'd reached the ripe old age of 969. Suddenly God looked down from heaven and said, "Well... I didn't want to do it, I've kept you alive **Methuselah** for a long, long, long time, longer than any other person because I didn't want to send my judgement on the planet, but the people just won't take any notice and the time has finally come."

And so that day **Methuselah** died. And it started raining.

So **Methuselah's** grandson, who was called Noah, took his family and lots of animals aboard the new boat, and God flooded the world and gave it a good wash.

And that's why **Methuselah** turned out to be the oldest man who ever lived, because as long as he was alive God would not send his judgement on the people, but as soon as he was dead the flood came. God really didn't want to send the flood, so he kept **Methuselah** alive as long as possible, but in the end there was just no other way out. And then his **name** turned out to be true - when he is dead it shall be sent. **Methuselah**.

Abraham and Sarah

Stars - All look up and shield eyes with hand
Cows - "Moo!"
Dogs - "Woof!"
Baby - All cry
Sand - Rub hands
Laughed - All laugh

A long time ago there was a man called Abraham. He had a wife called Sarah, and lots and lots of animals. Every night Abraham would stand outside and look up at the sky trying to count the **stars**. He would sit on the **sand**, with his **dogs**, and his **cows**. And one night as he was out there with the **stars** and the **sand** and the **dogs** and the **cows** - all of a sudden God appeared and said: "Abraham - you're wife is going to have a **baby**!" Well, Abraham was so surprised he nearly **laughed** because he and Sarah were very old and it was a shock to think they might have a **baby**. But the Lord told him that nothing is impossible for God to do and that Abraham and Sarah would have so many relatives that they wouldn't be able to count them all. In fact this one **baby** would become a great nation of people - more than all the **stars**, more than the grains of **sand**, and more than all the **dogs** and **cows**.

Well, Abraham thought about this for a long time - in fact, he thought about it every night as he sat out with the **stars** and the **sand** and the **dogs** and the **cows**. And sometimes he got quite excited about it. But a long, long time went by and they still didn't have a **baby**.
Then three visitors came to see him. And while they ate some tea, they said that quite soon Sarah would be a mother. When Sarah heard this she **laughed**... and **laughed**... and **laughed** - but sure enough a year later she had a **baby**!

And from then on every time they sat outside Abraham looked at the **stars**, and the **sand**, the **dogs** and the **cows**, and he remembered God's promise that one day he and Sarah would be the parents of a great nation.

Sodom and Gomorrah

Angry – Make an angry face and clench fists
Wrong – Cover face with hands and peep through fingers
Ordinary – "Really?"
Thud – "Bang!"
Bad – "Oh, oh!
Scary – Look scared, eyes wide

Sometimes we do things **wrong**, for all kinds of reasons.
Sometimes we do things **wrong** because we can't help it like...
Sometimes we do things **wrong** because we don't know how to do things right like...
And sometimes we do things **wrong** because we want to, like the story of Sodom and Gomorrah.
Sodom and Gomorrah were two cities. But these cities were not **ordinary**. Oh no…
They were full of people, but these people were not **ordinary**. Oh no…
They did lots of things, but the things they did were not **ordinary**. Oh no…
These people did lots of things **wrong**, not because they couldn't help it, not because they didn't know how to do things right, they did things **wrong** because they wanted to... and that made Sodom and Gomorrah very **scary** places to live in. Very **scary** indeed.

One day God sent a couple of his angels to visit Sodom. They arrived in the city as it was just getting dark, and they sat down in the city square. Just then a man called Lot came along. The angels were in disguise and the man didn't know who they were because they looked so **ordinary**. Oh yes.
"Hello," he said, "I haven't seen you here before, you're new here aren't you? Want to come to my house for a meal?"
"No, no, they said, "we like it here."
But Lot said, "No, come back to my place."
But they said, "No we're fine."
This went on for some time until the man said, "Please, pleeease, pleeeeease come back to my place."
So they went along with him.

They were just sitting down for an evening meal when there was a **thud** on the door.

It wasn't a nice gentle tap - instead it was a very loud **thud**!

"Open the door," shouted an **angry** voice, "we've seen those strangers."

One of the angels peeped outside through a crack in the door. They were surrounded by a mob of **angry** men, all shouting. It was very **scary**.

"It's the **bad** guys in the city. They'll do very **bad** things to you," said Lot.

"No they won't," said the angel and pushing the doors wide open he snapped his fingers and suddenly everyone outside couldn't see! And while the **bad** guys were wandering around, bashing into each other and falling over with a loud **thud**, the Angels took Lot and his family, and they ran as fast as they could away from the town. Suddenly they heard the sound of thunder. It was very, very, very **scary**.

"Don't look back," said the angels.

But Lot's wife did look back, and she saw the whole of Sodom being blown up by God. But it was **bad** news for her, as she watched her whole body turned into salt, and she was frozen there forever.

Abraham and Isaac

Mountain – Look, with hand above eyes
Understand – Scratch head and say "Mmm?"
Knife – Look shocked
Phew! – "Phew!"
Idea – Slap leg
Sacrifice/d – Hold out hands, palms upwards, as if holding up a sacrifice

Sometimes it's not easy to **understand** God. Like the time he asked Abraham to take his son out for a walk one day. "Let's go up that nice **mountain**," said Abraham.
And Isaac said, "Great **idea**, dad."
So off they went.
As they got near the top Abraham said, "Let's stop up the top and rest for a while."
And Isaac said, "Great **idea**, dad."
So up they went.
Up on top of the **mountain** they had an amazing view and Abraham suddenly said,
"I know let's give God a present, a **sacrifice** to tell him how good he is."
And Isaac said, "Great **idea**, dad."
So they got some wood together and got ready to set fire to it.
"What shall we use for the **sacrifice**?" Isaac asked.
And Abraham thought for a while and said, "I know – you!"
And Isaac said, "Er… Great **idea**? Dad?"

Sometimes it's not easy to **understand** God. He had given Abraham a precious son and now he had told Abraham to kill him. It seemed very unfair.
Abraham looked very sad as he lifted Isaac up as a **sacrifice** and laid him gently on the wood.
Isaac looked very confused.
Then Abraham took out his **knife**, lifted it up in the air and brought it down on Isaac.

"Stop!" yelled a voice, and at the last minute Abraham's **knife** stopped right over Isaac's heart.

It was an angel.

"Don't kill the boy," said the angel. "Look there's a ram over there you can use that for the **sacrifice**, now that God can see you are prepared to obey him even to the point of killing your own son, you don't have to do it. Well done, Abraham, you put God first."

And Abraham killed the ram instead and **sacrificed** that on the fire.

And Isaac said, "**Phew!**"

And he looked very relieved.

Jacob's Wrestling Match

Jacob – All girls stand
Esau – All boys stand
Father/Dad – All fathers stand
Mother – All mothers stand
Wife – Any married women stand
Brother – Any brothers stand
Sons – All sons stand
Family – Everyone stand
(Suggestion: Deliberately mispronounce *smoothie* in verse two
so that it rhymes with *toothy*)

Jacob had a brother, **Esau** was his name,
They didn't get on very well, they just weren't the same

Jacob was a gentle man, **Esau** was rough and toothy,
Esau was a hairy man, **Jacob** was a smoothie.

Esau was his **father's** favourite; **Jacob** was his **mother's**,
Jacob's mum persuaded him to pinch what was his **brother's**.

Jacob went to see his **dad**, disguised in skin pyjamas
His **father** gave him a blessing and **Esau** went bananas.

So **Jacob** did a runner, he had to get away
He left behind the **family**, in total disarray.

Years went by and before too long a **wife** or two he had
He also had eleven **sons**, and they all called him **dad**.

It was time to go back home, though **Jacob** was terrified
The last time he saw **Esau**, he'd threatened fratricide… er what's
fratricide?
(Ask audience then continue)

The night before they met - a strange thing came to pass
God came to earth for **Jacob** and they had a wrestling match.

All night long the fight went on, but **Jacob** wouldn't slip.
As dawn approached God said, "Let me go," and he struck him on the hip.

"Your name will not be **Jacob**," said God, "it's Israel from now on.
You've wrestled with both man and God, and I'm surprised to say you've won."

And God blessed **Jacob** there and then, and **Jacob** knelt and said,
"Wow! I have met God face to face and I should now be dead."

Then **Jacob** left that place and went limping on his way,
And **Esau**, when 'e saw his **brother**… he didn't blow him away.

The two forgave each other and went back home that night.
"Where'd you get that limp?" asked **Esau**, and **Jacob** said, "A fight."

Frisk & Dexter and the Boy in the Well

Mean - "Grrrrr!"
Dangerous - "Oh! Oh!" and look scared
Colours - "Zing!"
Well - Squelching mud sound
Coat - Pull up collar
Notebook - Flick open

Frisk and Dexter ran a time travel investigation agency. They were detectives who could investigate any crime from any time. When the purple phone on Dexter's desk rang like an old school bell, they knew that a case from history was calling them. Dexter wore a long black **coat** and had a dog called Bilko. Frisk wore small, dark glasses and always carried a **notebook**. One day the purple phone rang...
And Frisk and Dexter found themselves sweating in the middle of a hot desert, Frisk was grateful for his dark glasses as the sun beat down like a massive spotlight, but Dexter threw of his long black **coat** and left it lying in the dust. They began to walk.

"Where now, boss?" asked Frisk, flicking open his **notebook** and beginning to scribble in it.
"Listen!" Dexter stopped in his tracks so that Frisk walked into him, and Bilko walked into Frisk.
"Shhh!" said Dexter, they listened and heard the sound of a cry, Frisk pointed to an old muddy **well** and they ran towards it like kids running for an ice cream van. They stopped and looked in, a young teenager lay at the bottom, his body crunched up and splashes of blood smeared on his face and clothes. The situation looked **dangerous**.
"Someone's thrown him in," whispered Frisk, still scribbling in his **notebook**.
"Why are you whispering?" whispered Dexter.
They looked around, the place was deserted.
"Sorry," said Frisk, "thought the guys who threw him in might still be around."

Dexter tried to reach inside to pull the boy out, but the **well** was too deep.
"Here boss, try this," Frisk had picked up Dexter's black **coat**. They
lowered it into the **well** for the boy to grab hold of, but it was still too
short.
"Nothing else for it," said Dexter, rolling his sleeves up, "I'm going in."
"No wait!"
Just as he was about to climb inside Frisk pointed off into the distance, a
long wiry line of camels appeared on the skyline. The riders looked **mean**,
and **dangerous**.
"No time to waste," said Dexter, "If we don't get him, they will."

But Frisk stopped him again. He pointed down inside the **well**, towards a
torn piece of the boy's **coat**. It lay next to him and it was all the **colours** of
the rainbow.
"I don't think we should rescue him, Boss," said Frisk, "I think this boy's
gonna go to Egypt and get a top job in government."
Dexter wasn't so sure. He looked at the **coat** with all its **colours**, then at the
line of camels.
"They look **mean**," he said, "could be **dangerous**."
"It'll be all right," said Frisk, "look - here come the boy's brothers."
Ten men were approaching the **well** from nowhere.
"Help!" said Dexter, "let's get back to the future, quick!"
As they ran back to the 90's, Frisk noted in his book that sometimes it was
better to leave things for God to work out...

Moses Runs Away

Divide audience into five sections, each one representing a different
character or set of characters.
Moses – Section one stand
Pharaoh – Section two stand
Soldier – Section three stand
Workers - Section four stand
Sheep/Lambs - Section five stand

Moses was a Prince in Egypt, he was dead, dead rich
He lived it up in **Pharaoh**'s palace without a hitch or glitch.

One day **Moses** went outside walking round the city
There were a lot of **workers** working, and the place was not too pretty.

Then he saw a **soldier** hit one of the men at work
Moses wasn't pleased with this and he went berserk.

Moses ran up to the **soldier**, and hit him on the head
It hurt his hand, and **Moses** groaned, the **soldier** fell down dead.

The **soldier** lay there in the dirt, dead upon the sand,
Moses was in big trouble, and he had a bad hand.

Moses dug a pit and buried the **soldier** in the sun.
Then he went home to the palace and tried to forget just what he'd done.

Next day **Moses** went out and he saw two **workers** fight,
"Stop that," said **Moses**, "don't argue - that's not right."

The **workers** took one look at him and started to back away.
"Don't kill us please," they begged him, "like that **soldier** yesterday."

Moses' face went white and his mouth filled with his heart.
Everyone knew what he had done and it wasn't very smart.

"Excuse me," **Moses** said, and he turned and ran away.
He ran and ran and ran and ran and didn't stop all day.

That was the end of **Moses'** career after causing such a rumpus,
He got another job - tending **sheep** and woolly jumpers.

But God was still in charge and things were not all they seemed.
While Moses cared for **lambs** – he was on a training scheme.

Years later **Moses** went back to Egypt and set the **workers** free
Moses made an awful fuss and he spoilt **Pharaoh's** tea.

God opened up the river Nile and the **workers** ran away.
But **Pharaoh's soldiers** -they got drowned – it wasn't their day.

Ten Good Rules

Desert - Fan face and say "Are we there yet?"
Mountain – Form a mountain shape with hands and arms
Good – Make a thumbs up sign
Any numbers – Hold up appropriate number on fingers

While Moses was leading the people of Israel across the **desert** they came to a **mountain** and while the people had a rest Moses went up the **mountain** and had a talk with God. And said, here are **ten good** rules for living well.

Rule number **one**: Nothing and no one is more important than God.

Rule number **two**: Make God number one in your life and let everything else come second.

Number **three**: God's name is special and sacred, don't use it as a swear word.

Number **four**: Remember that Sunday is God's special day.

Number **five**: Respect your family and those who take care of you.

Number **six**: Don't kill.

Number **seven**: Only sleep with your husband or wife.

Number **eight**: Don't steal

Number **nine**: Don't tell lies.

Number **ten**: Don't look at what your friend has and wish it were yours.

To sum it all up, love God and treat others the way you would like them to treat you.

God wrote all these things down for Moses whilst he was up the **mountain**, then he went back down the **mountain** to tell the people in the **desert** about the **ten good** rules for living well.

Samuel in the Temple

Candles - All blow twice
Cat - "Miaow"
Door - "Click, click"
Stairs - Footsteps followed by snoring sounds
Heard - Call out "Samuel!"

Once upon a time there was a young boy called Samuel.
He used to work in the temple, helping Eli who was the priest there. Every night it was Samuel's job to blow out the **candles** on the altar; lock up the front **door**; put the **cat** out the back door; and then he would climb the **stairs** to bed.

Late one night, after he'd blown out the **candles**; locked up the **door;** put out the **cat**; and climbed the **stairs** to bed; the Lord God spoke to Samuel. This is what he **heard**...

Samuel was amazed when he **heard**… so he hurried down the **stairs**; checked the **cat**; checked the **door**; checked the **candles**; then he woke up Eli, who said:
"Samuel, do you know what time it is? It's way past your bedtime and you've got to be up early tomorrow. Now go back to bed."
So Samuel went back up the **stairs** to bed.

Just then he **heard**... so he hurried back down the **stairs**; checked the **cat**; the **door**; and the **candles**; and then he went to Eli, who said: "Samuel, you're worse than a faulty alarm clock. Go back to bed." So Samuel went back up**stairs** to bed. Once again he **heard**...

This time Samuel ran down the **stairs** and went straight to Eli. And this time Eli realised it was the Lord who was calling to Samuel. So Eli said: "Next time the Lord calls you, tell him you are listening and ask Him to speak to you." And that's exactly what Samuel did, and after that God did speak to him, many times. And as he grew older, God used Samuel as a leader to guide and help people.

Queen Esther

Divide the audience into five sections, each section representing one of the characters listed below. They stand then sit down quickly again.

Esther – Stand and punch the air
Xerxes – Stand with hands on hips, as if in charge
Vashti/Zeresh – Stand and tut, unimpressed
Haman – Stand and look down nose, snobby
Mordecai – Stand and stroke chin wisely

In a lot of the Bible stories we read, the Bible tells us what God is doing – the story of Esther is quite different. We only hear about what is happening down here on earth.

Xerxes was a King, a fairly brutal lout.
He said, "My dear wife **Vashti**, has turned a bit nasty,
So I think I'll throw her out."
So poor old **Vashti** got the boot, King **Xerxes** was not nice.
Then **Xerxes** said, "I'll have a new wife instead.
But I won't make the same mistake twice."

Xerxes ruled 100 kingdoms, from India to Sudan
They searched his world for the perfect girl
For this very imperfect man.
Now **Mordecai** he was a Jew and **Esther** was his niece
He worked for the king and soon got wind
Of his search for wedded bliss.

Mordecai said, "Listen my young **Esther**, I'd like to propose a motion,
I've foreseen, that you're gonna be queen.
Now that's quite a promotion."
Esther was quite young but she also was quite bright,
She went to **Xerxes** with bows and curtsies,
And he fell in love at first sight.

Now **Haman** was Prime Minister he wasn't half a snob
He said, "My wife **Zeresh**, I no longer cherish
Half as much as my job."
He also wasn't very keen on **Mordecai** the Jew,
Because when he went by, old **Mordecai**
Didn't bow the way the others would do.

"Right," he said, "I will not have it, **Mordecai**'s bad news.
I'll trick the king into killing him
Along with all the Jews."
So **Xerxes** signed an order sealing **Mordecai**'s fate
Haman had a grin, but **Zeresh** put in,
 "It ain't over yet, just wait."

When **Mordecai** heard the news he ran to **Esther**'s pad,
He fell on his knees and said, "**Esther** please
King **Xerxes** has gone quite mad."
Mordecai explained and poor old **Esther** said:
 "**Haman**'s nasty, bring back **Vashti** –
Let her be queen instead."

"I can't change anything," she said, "but I'll do the best I can."
She fasted and prayed for three whole days
And then she had a plan.
She gave the King a party, **Haman**, and **Zeresh** were there too
As they got under way, **Esther** started to say,
"King **Xerxes**, **Haman**'s tricked you."

Xerxes was so surprised he backed out through the door,
Haman grabbed **Esther**, tripped up and pressed her
Flat upon the floor.
Xerxes walked back in just then, a snarl upon his lips.
Zeresh tutted, **Xerxes** was gutted,
He said, "**Haman**'s had his chips."

So **Haman** got the chop - his evil plans forsaken.
The Jews all blessed her, good old **Esther**
She had saved their bacon.

Job's Troubles

Divide audience into five sections, each one representing a different character or set of characters. You could add appropriate noises.

Job – Section one stand
Children – Section two stand
Servants – Section three stand
Friends- Section four stand
Animals (Sheep, cows and camels) - Section five stand

Job lived in the land of Uz
He was a very rich man,
He had ten **children** and many **servants**,
Cows and **sheep** and land.

They often had big parties
They'd feast and laugh all night.
But **Job** would always speak to God
In the early morning light.

Job prayed for all his **children**
And cared for them every one,
But he was not prepared
For the havoc that was to come.

One afternoon a **servant**
Came running and out of breath.
"We have been attacked," he said,
"And your **servants** put to death."

A second **servant** then appeared
Breathless and covered in mud.
He said, "A storm has killed your **sheep**…
The field's are red with blood."

Before he could finish talking
Another **servant** came to say,
"A band of rebels attacked from the north
And they've taken your **camels** away."

Before this one could end his message
A fourth came up and said,
"Sir, a tornado has struck nearby
And all your **children** are dead."

"This is terrible news," said **Job**,
"My life's become a ruin.
I don't know why God has allowed this,
But he must know what he's doing."

"He gave me everything I had,
And now he's taken it away."
And **Job** went off and prayed to God.
And fell ill the very next day.

But still **Job** would not blame God,
He would not curse or shout.
Some of **Job's friends** heard he was ill
So they came to sort him out.

When his **friends** saw **Job** they were shocked.
They sighed and stroked their chins.
"God must be very upset," they said,
"Because of all your sins."

The **friends** gave lots of reasons
Why things had gone so wrong.
But they didn't know what they were talking about
So they left… and God came along.

"Why's this happened?" said **Job**, at last,
"Why? It's just not fair.
I've lost **children**, **servants**, **sheep** and **cows**
Yet you don't seem to care."

So God showed **Job** the clouds,
The mountains, sea, and land.
He said, "Did you do all this, I don't think so,
This came from the work of my hand."

"I am the creator of all things,
And you are just a man.
And though you're kind and generous
There are things you can't understand."

Job was ashamed of his ranting,
He fell down and knelt in the dust.
God said, "I won't give you an answer, **Job**,
But I'll restore everything you have lost."

Jeremiah and the Potter

Knock – Knock on floor or chair
Word – Place hand to ear and listen
Instructions – "I see."
Potter/s – Watch imaginary potter's wheel go round
Clay – "Splat!" And mime throwing a lump of clay on a potter's wheel
Hands – Pretend to mould clay with hands

One day Jeremiah was relaxing at home. When suddenly…
There was a **knock** at the door.
It was the Lord.
"Jeremiah," he said, "I want a **word** with you."
And Jeremiah said, "Who me?"
And the Lord said: "Yes, I want a **word** with you."

And the Lord gave Jeremiah some very interesting **instructions**.
He said, "I want you to go down to the **potter's** house."
"The **potter's** house?" said Jeremiah. And the Lord said, "YES!!"
So Jeremiah took note of these **instructions** and off he went.
At the **potter's** house he watched the **potter** at work, moulding his **clay**
with his **hands**.

Whenever the piece of **clay** he was working with turned out wrong -
The potter scrunched it up in his **hands** and threw away the **clay**.

Oh no, I'm sorry, I got that wrong, he <u>didn't</u> throw it away.
No.
Instead, he remoulded the **clay** into something else. Something new. And
the Lord said to Jeremiah: "You are in my **hands**. And I have the right to
remould you."

Louder than Words

People – All wave
Dung – Poo! Wave hand in front of face
Hair – Snip snip
Clothes – "Ha!" Shocked
Rucksack – Sing: "Hi ho, hi ho…"
Really – All nod emphatically

Way, way back, a long time ago there was a good old prophet called Ezekiel. He used to tell **people** what God was thinking – but he didn't use words. Oh no, he used to act out the messages that God told him.

One day God told Ezekiel about a battle, so Ezekiel made a model of the town and he acted out the battle.
Another time God told Ezekiel to cut his **hair** and divide the **hair** into three parts. So Ezekiel did that. The three bundles of **hair** were like the **people** and Ezekiel was showing them what would happen to each of them.
Another time he asked Ezekiel to pack a **rucksack** and pretend to sneak out of his house with the **rucksack** as if he was running away. This was to show the people how they would have to escape from the city.
Another time God told Ezekiel to walk around without wearing any **clothes**!

But the strangest thing of all was when God told Ezekiel to make some bread and bake it on a fire made out of human **dung**!
Ezekiel had done lots of things but this time he argued about it, and said, "I can't do that Lord, it's horrible, and I'm sure that you would think it's horrible too. I can't believe you **really** want me to do that. Not on human **dung**."
And God said, "**Really**, I do."
Ezekiel said, "**Really**?"
And God said, "**Really**."
And Ezekiel said, "**Really, really, really**?"
And God said, "**Really, really, really**."

In the end God said, "Okay, you can cook it on a fire of cow **dung** if you want instead. You know, Ezekiel, sometimes I'm prepared to go much further than you think to reach **people**."

So Ezekiel did all these amazing things to communicate God's message to the **people** but a lot of them didn't listen, so in the end, years later, God went to the absolute limit to communicate with **people** – he became a man and died for them.

Daniel in the Lions' Den

Daniel - All cheer
Pray/Prayed - Shout "Amen!"
Lions – "Roar!"
King/King's men – "Hissss!"
Went - Make the sound of running steps

Once upon a time there was a man called **Daniel**.
He was a man who worshipped God and **prayed** to Him three times every day. But the **king,** who **Daniel** worked for, didn't worship God, or **pray** to Him.

And one day, some of the **king's men**, who'd been watching **Daniel**, thought of a plan to get rid of him, because the **king's men** didn't like him. So, they **went** to the **king** and made him write out an order telling all the people that for one month they must only worship the **king** and no one else, and if they did they would be thrown to the **lions** and eaten.

When **Daniel** heard this, he wasn't worried went off to his room to **pray**, three times just like he always did.
When the **king's men** found out, they forced the **king** to throw Daniel into the **lions'** den.
But **Daniel** was a man of faith and he believed that God would look after him. And you know what?
God did look after him. For one whole night the **lions** never touched **Daniel** they completely lost their appetites and became vegetarians.

When the **king** saw this he let **Daniel** out of the **lions'** den, and ordered that everyone should worship God; and **pray** to Him whenever they wanted to.

The Shepherds

Shepherds - "Ooh aarr!"
Angel - "Alleluia"
Sheep - Baa!
Bright - Flick fingers out and say "Whoosh!"
Stable - Sniff twice and say "Ugh!"
Baby - Suck thumb or say "Aah!"

While **shepherds** watched their **sheep** one night
All seated on the ground,
An **angel** in the sky appeared
And **bright** light shone around.

"Fear not!" The **angel** said, for they were
Scared out of their minds.
"I've got good news - the future's **bright**
For you and all mankind."

The **angel** said: "In Bethlehem
A **baby's** just been born;
His name is Jesus - and he will be,
Your helper, friend and Lord!

You'll find this little **baby**
In a **stable** made of wood;
He'll be wrapped up in an animal trough
And the place won't smell too good!"

And when the **angel** took a break
A million more turned up -
All shining **bright** and singing strong,
And praising God above.

Then all the **shepherds** left their **sheep**
And ran into the town -
They walked in circles trying to find out
What was going down.

They saw a **stable** lit up **bright**
Just like a Christmas tree.
They all rushed over, crept inside,
And dropped on bended knee.

The parents of the **baby** there -
They looked surprised and stressed.
The **shepherds** grinned; the **baby** stared,
The **sheep** were not impressed.

All the **shepherds** worshipped him
Then went back to their **sheep**.
The **baby** in the **stable** yawned
And just went back to sleep!

And since that time of **sheep** and **shepherds**;
And **stables** shining **bright**;
The **baby** has become a king -
And what the **angel** said - was right...

Christmas Crowd Story

Suitable for an outdoor or large event, the responses are fairly noisy, like those in a pantomime.

Baby – Divide audience in two (1&2): 1."Gurgle, gurgle,"
2. "Howl, howl," 1. "Gurgle, gurgle," 2. "Howl, howl."
Camels –All say "Brrrr" and make lips vibrate for camel sounds
Innkeeper – Cough and clear throat noisily
Shepherds – "Baaa!"
Kings – Salute and bow quickly
Stable – Creaking noises

This is the story of Christmas
2000 years ago,
With **camels** and **innkeepers** and **shepherds**,
But no sign of any snow.

Come back with me to Palestine
Back to the Middle East,
With **camels, innkeepers** and **shepherds**
And the ancient Prince of Peace.

Late one cold dark night
Some **shepherds** came to town,
They came upon an inn
And nearly broke the front door down.

The **innkeeper** was a gruff old sort
In scruffy clothes and shoes,
"You can't stay here," he told 'em.
And he didn't half smell of booze.

They'd come to see the **baby**
The one out in the **stable,**
They'd heard that he was special
And didn't think it was no fable.

They went around the back
To the **stable** and the hay
And there amongst the cow dung
A tiny **baby** lay.

Later on some rich blokes
Came riding on their travels,
They were **kings** and wise men
And they all rode on **camels**.

They'd come to see the **baby**
Those **kings** they were pretty clever
"We won't forget this child," they said,
"And you should call him Trevor."

They didn't call him Trevor
But they were right about one thing,
No one forgot the child that night -
He turned out to be a **king**.

When He Appeared

Tiny – Hold hands a few inches apart, showing how small the baby was
Mother – Pat stomach   **Eyes wide** – Open eyes wide in wonder
Spices – Rub fingers and sniff   **Gold** – "Wow!"
News – Whisper to person next to you
Light – Point upwards, say "Ha!" in wonder

When he appeared they expected a warrior,
An angel of **light**, or a king.
Not a **tiny** baby, wrapped in straw,
No one expected him.

A fodder trough, a stable and stars,
A teenage **mother**-to-be.
Was this the way to change things?
Was this way it should be?

So he was born, in the dust and the dung,
A **tiny** child of the night.
Shepherds knelt, **eyes wide**
And men from the East saw the **light**.

Both rich and poor were assembled there
Kneeling beside the child and his **mother**
The kings brought gifts of **spices** and **gold**
The shepherds just brought each other.

Quietly they rose and left that place,
Whispered goodbyes were exchanged in the street
The kings went abroad to pass on the **news**
The shepherds went home for a bite to eat.

And two thousand years have since come and gone
And each one remembered the child in the night
The shepherds and kings have long disappeared
But the baby lives on, turning darkness to **light**.

Frisk & Dexter and the Bad King

Investigate - Mime looking through a magnifying glass
Baby – Mime holding a baby
Soldier/Soldiers - Hold spear, curl lip and look mean
Yelled/Yelling - Open mouth wide
Stable – Sniff loudly
Straw - Crinkle, rustle, crinkle rustle

Frisk and Dexter ran a time travel **investigation** agency. They were detectives who could **investigate** any crime from any time. When the purple phone on Dexter's desk rang like an old school bell, they knew that a case from history was calling them. Dexter wore a long black **coat** and had a dog called Bilko. Frisk wore small, dark glasses and always carried a notebook. One day the purple phone rang...

And Frisk and Dexter found themselves back in time, standing in a big busy city. Dexter pulled a file from his pocket; it said "The Case of the Bad King".
He looked inside.
"Look at this," he said. "It says King Herod is accused of the terrible crime of killing innocent **babies**."
Frisk jotted this down in his notebook, then he pointed across the street.
"Let's ask that **soldier** if he knows where Herod lives," he said.

They walked over. But before they could **investigate** the **soldier** lifted his spear and pushed them away.
"Get back!" he **yelled**. "This is official business."
Frisk and Dexter backed away just as another **soldier** came out of a nearby house. He nodded at the other **soldier** and they walked off.
Frisk went over to the house and looked inside. A man and a woman were standing inside looking very scared.
"What's going on?" Frisk asked.
"Those soldiers wanted to arrest our children," said the man.
"Why?" asked Dexter.

"We don't know, they're arresting all the children who are two or under," said the woman. "Our two children are three and four, so they went away." Frisk and Dexter promised they would **investigate** and they went back outside.

"Look," yelled Dexter, and he pointed at the **soldiers**' footprints in the dust. "Let's follow these guys."

So they took up the trail. They found the **soldiers** in the next street, Dexter pulled Frisk back into the shadows and they watched as the men went from house to house looking for the children. Then there was a terrible scream from one of the houses and the **soldiers** came out with a **baby** in their arms. Quick as a flash Dexter leapt forward and rugby tackled the one with the **baby**. Frisk in the meantime hurled his notebook at the other soldier, **yelling,** "Catch!" to distract him. Dexter jumped to his feet and grabbed the **baby** from the **soldier**.

"Run!" he **yelled** and so they did.

Frisk and Dexter ran and ran and ran like mad. Behind them the **soldiers** ran too, but their armour slowed them down and before long Frisk and Dexter had got away. They found themselves outside an old deserted **stable**. They went inside and collapsed in a heap. Dexter looked for somewhere safe to put the **baby**. Frisk pointed at an animal trough and they filled it with **straw** and some old cloth and laid the **baby** in it.

As they watched it lying in the **straw** Dexter snapped his fingers.

"I know what this is all about," he said, "look at this **stable**. This is the place where Jesus was born. And Herod is scared of him, because he's going to be a king, so he's trying to kill all the new-born **babies**."

"So it's true," said Frisk, "Herod did commit those terrible murders." They scooped up the **baby** and crept back outside.

"Come on," said Dexter, "there's nothing we can do to stop this. Herod is a bad king, if we're careful we might just save this one. Let's see if it's safe to take the **baby** back to its parents, and then we'd better get back to the future."

And they left the old **stable** behind and ran back to the town... It was a very sad case indeed.

Jesus in the Temple

by Soobie Whitfield

Travel/Travelled - "Trudge, trudge" With arm swings
Worried - Bite nails
People - "Rhubarb, rhubarb"
Temple - (Sing) "A-a-amen"
Searching/Searched - Hands over eyes, call "Jesus, Jesus?"
Donkey/s - "Eeaw!"

Passover was an exciting time of year. All the Jewish **people travelled** to Jerusalem to say thank you to God for helping them to escape from their enemies. It was a long journey. The road was very busy with **donkey**s carrying supplies. The **people** walked in family groups. Some of the younger children soon grew hot and tired and were picked up by their parents and put on the **donkeys**' backs.

Mary, Joseph and Jesus **travelled** this journey every year.   Jesus was now twelve years old and big enough to guide their **donkey** through the crowds of **people**. Once they reached Jerusalem everyone was heading for one place - the **temple**. The **temple** stood on a great hillside and looked magnificent. Inside it was even more amazing. Many **people** had worked hard to make it a beautiful place for worshipping God.   Inside the Jewish teachers sat and taught the **people** about God.

This year because there were so many **people** Jesus got separated from his parents in the crowd. But he wasn't **worried** because he knew where the **temple** was. He loved it there and happily guided the **donkey** inside until he found a safe place to tie her up and leave her. Then he crept into the **temple** and joined the celebrations.

Once the Passover celebrations had finished all the **people** returned home. Some were quite sad because it was the end of their holiday, but they collected their baggage and their **donkey**s and **travelled** homewards. Because there were so many **people**, Mary and Joseph didn't notice that Jesus was missing. They thought that he was with some of his friends. However, after the first night came and he hadn't rejoined them Mary started to worry. Their **donkey** was missing too - with all their food and blankets. By dawn Mary and Joseph were **searching** for Jesus everywhere. But the more they searched the more **worried** they became. Finally one of the **people** suggested that they should **travel** back to Jerusalem.

Mary and Joseph ran all the way back to the city. As they came close to the **temple** they saw that there were still lots of **people** in the streets talking and laughing. "Look over there!" said Joseph, and he pointed to a small brown **donkey** tied to a post. It was theirs, but where was Jesus? Joseph climbed the steps to the **temple** and as he entered the courtyards saw Jesus talking to the **temple** teachers in a shaded corner.

When Joseph returned with Jesus to his mother she was quite angry. "Why have you done this?" she said, "We were so **worried** about you." Jesus was puzzled. "Why were you **searching** for me? Didn't you know I would be in my Father's house?" For Jesus was the Son of God - and he wanted to be close to his Father in the **temple**. Mary didn't quite understand Jesus - but she remembered what he said.

Talking to God

This is more of a copy sketch than a response story, i.e. one person reads the narrative and another person, or group of people, leads the congregation in simple mimed responses.

Our Father in heaven: (Look up, like a child to a parent)

Hallowed be your name, (Run hands over large imaginary name plaque hanging above and in front of you)

Your Kingdom come;
Your will be done (Raise an ear to heaven as if listening for God's guidance)

On earth as it is in heaven. (Reach down and scoop up some earth, rub it with fingers)

Give us this day our daily bread. (Tip away the earth and with both hands lift up a bread roll and tear it in two, mime eating a chunk)

And forgive us our sins, (Cup right hand as if holding sins, look into it then raise it out front and to your right)

As we forgive those who
sin against us. (Cup left hand, look at this then hold that out, so that you are balancing left and right, like scales. Turn both hands over and let all the sins go)

Lead us not into temptation, (Reach out for something, then stop and retract hand)

But deliver us from evil.	(Hold hands up to shield face from danger)
For yours is the kingdom,	(Sweep hands together in front of you as if collecting up a large bundle)
The power,	(Lift the imaginary bundle up high - just as God has the power to carry us)
And the glory,	(Sweep hands across and above you as if smoothing out the sky)
Forever and ever,	(Remove watch from wrist and throw it away)
Amen.	(Bow heads, with hands clasped)

Jesus Spoils a Funeral

Sad/Saddest – Pull a sad face
Gasp – "Ha!"
Walked/Walking – Make walking movement in your seat
Crowd – "That's us!"

One day, as Jesus was walking along, he and his friends came to a town and found a long line of people all **walking** along and looking down at the ground. Their faces were very **sad**.
"What's wrong?" Jesus asked, "Why do they all look so sad?"
The people **walked** in silence, looking down at the ground, and the **saddest** of them all was a little old lady.
One of Jesus' friends went off to find out what it was all about, and when he came he said, "It's a funeral, that lady is a widow and she's lost her only son, she's all on her own now."
As they watched the long procession of people **walking** past it was such a **sad** sight that Jesus suddenly held up a hand and said, "Wait a minute, there must be something we can do here."

He pushed through the **crowd** until he got close to the old lady.
"Please don't cry," he said, "it's not over yet."
The old lady looked confused, but she did stop crying for a moment and watched as Jesus **walked** up to her son as he lay in the coffin.
The coffin was being carried by some men who stopped **walking** when they saw Jesus. They put it down and Jesus looked at the boy lying in side it. Jesus looked around at the large **crowd** who were staring at him, he gave a little smile and then he looked down at the boy and said, "Young man, get up! Now!"
There was a shocked **gasp** from the **crowd** and for a moment nothing happened. Then, slowly the boy opened one eye, then the other. He yawned and coughed and sat up.
The **crowd** gave another **gasp** and some of them fell over, they were so shocked.
Suddenly the boy began talking to his mother, the **crowd** gave another **gasp** and even more of them fell over.

The boy climbed out of the coffin and gave his mother big hug. Suddenly everyone was laughing and crying and shouting and running about.

As Jesus and his friends **walked** away they heard people in the **crowd** shouting, " This is amazing! That man must be some kind of great prophet! God's come to save us!"
Jesus smiled to himself again; he'd spoilt a funeral but saved a life. It was good day.

Up the Mountain

Get the audience to click their fingers, or clap their hands in a rap rhythm. They should repeat the last line of each verse twice so you may like to teach these at the beginning.

Peter, James and his brother John,
They were all fishing men.
One day Jesus said to them:
"Follow me and you'll catch men!"

All: "Follow me and you'll catch men!" x 2

So they followed him, became his friend -
Jesus did miracles - lots of them.
Then one day he said to them:
"Come with me and meet my friends."

All: "Come with me and meet my friends." x 2

Peter, John and his brother James
Found themselves on a mountain range!
Suddenly Jesus began to change,
James and John felt very strange!

All: James and John felt very strange! x 2

Jesus' face was all alight,
And his clothes were whiter than white.
He looked dazzling - shining bright.
Peter was shaking, full of fright.

All: Peter was shaking, full of fright. x 2

Just then two more men appeared,
In sandals, cloaks and very long beards.
Peter spoke up, still full of fear,
Said: "It's really great to be up here!"

All: "It's really great to be up here!" x 2

"I know," said Pete, "let's build three tents
For Jesus and those other two gents."
A cloud appeared - it didn't make sense.
It came from nowhere - foggy and dense.

All: It came from nowhere - foggy and dense. x 2

It covered them all from head to foot
And then a voice said: "Listen out!
This is my son, without a doubt,
I'm pleased with him so hear him out."

All: I'm pleased with him so hear him out." x 2

Peter, James and his brother John
Were terrified and all fell down.
Jesus put his hand on them, said:
"Don't be afraid - everyone's gone!"

All: "Don't be afraid - everyone's gone!" x 2

They looked up - saw no one around,
And they were glad to get back to town.
Jesus said: "Don't forget what you saw,
And later on you'll see some more."

All: Later on you'll see some more." x 2

Teaching, Healing, Miracles and Stories

Teaching – Place hands out, open as if talking
Healing – Place hands together as if praying
Miracles – Snap fingers
Stories – Listen, hand to ear
Good – Punch the air
Dust – Dust hands off
Fantastic - Cheer

After Jesus had been travelling about a lot, **teaching** people, **healing** them, doing **miracles** and telling **stories** he decided it was time for his friends to have a go.

First of all he sent out his twelve closest friends.
He said, "Go out to all the people in the nearby villages and towns, **teaching** them, **healing** those who are sick, doing **miracles** and telling them **stories**."
The disciples were a bit worried about this.
They said, "You're the one who does that, Jesus, not us. You're good at it, why don't you do it? And we'll walk behind you."
But Jesus said, "It's your turn, don't take anything with you, don't bother about packing lots of nice things, or emptying your bank accounts, just go quickly and simply, and wherever you meet people who welcome you, stay with them, **teaching**, **healing**, doing **miracles** and telling **stories**."
"So people will like us and treat us nicely?"
"Of course,"
"Oh **good**," said his friends.
"Yes, and when they don't shake the **dust** off your feet and leave them."
"What d'you mean, Lord, when they don't? Isn't this going to be easy then?"
"No, but off you go."
So they nervously went.

When they got back Jesus' friends were over the moon.
"We did it," they said. "It was **fantastic**."

"Good," said Jesus, "I'm sending you out again, this time with a lot more friends. Seventy two of you."

"Oh that's **good**," they said.

"Yes," said Jesus, "I'm sending you out like lambs among wolves,"

"Oh dear, that's bad," they said, "that's not exactly a word of encouragement Lord."

And Jesus said, "There is a large harvest but only a few people to gather it in. Pray that there will be lots and lots more workers. You'll need more than twelve, more than seventy-two. And remember when you meet people who welcome you, stay with them, **teaching**, **healing**, doing **miracles** and telling **stories**."

"We like that bit," they said.

"Yes. And when they don't, shake the **dust** off your feet."

"We don't like that bit," they said, but they went off, nervous yet again.

When they got back, Jesus' friends said, "Lord, it was **fantastic**!"

And Jesus said, "**Good**. But remember, even though you've done amazing things the most important thing is that you and I are best friends."

A Good Harvest

Seeds - Mime throwing seeds with right hand and say "Whoosh!"
Ground - Stamp feet on floor once
Concrete - "Dong!" and hit fist on head
Soil - Rub fingers together and say "Squelch, squelch!"
Yobs - Shout "Oi!!"
Thorns - "Ouch!"
Day - Yawn and stretch at the start of a new day

A man went out to sow some **seeds**.
He ploughed the field and scattered
The **seeds** fell on the **ground**
But some of them got splattered.

Some **seeds** fell on hard **ground**
The soil was just like **concrete**
And the local **yobs** jumped on them
With big boots on their big feet.

Some **seeds** fell in **thorns**
"Ouch!" the **seeds** did cry.
But no one came to help them
And soon the **seeds** did die.

Some **seeds** fell on thin **soil**
And couldn't grow too high
And when the sun came out that **day**
Those little **seeds** did fry!

A man went out to sow some **seeds**
He ploughed the field and scattered.
Some **seeds** fell on juicy **soil**
And that's what really mattered.

The **seeds** are just like words from God
We hear them every **day**
We see God out there in the world -
At home, at work, at play.

We can be like **concrete** and
God's word will bounce away
Or we can be like juicy **soil**
And grow a little more each day.

We don't have to be so big
To grow a bit each **day**,
And when the **thorns** and **yobs** come round
We can turn to God and say:
"Help!"

The Parable of the Lost Golf Ball

Not – "Oh oh!" (Sounding worried)
Rough – "Ouch!"
Golf ball – "Thwack!"
Pete – One half of audience stand
Sid – Other half stand

Once upon a time two men met for a game of golf. One was a professional player – the other was **not**!
The professional was called **Pete** – Professional **Pete** they all called him. He was the smoothest, fastest, slickest golfer in the entire district.
The other was **not**.
The other man was called **Sid**, Slowhand **Sid** they all called him. He was the slowest, silliest, most unprofessional golfer in the entire universe.
Professional **Pete** had won every game he'd played in the last ten years. Slowhand **Sid** had **not**.

Well, they met bright and early one morning, shook hands and teed off. **Pete** started with a hole in one, **Sid** did **not**. He started by hitting his **ball** into the bunker. From there he hit into the lake and from there he knocked it into the **rough** and lost it.
So he gave up on that hole and they went onto hole number two. **Pete** won that one too, and in fact, he won the first ten they played. Things were **not** looking good for **Sid**.

Then, suddenly, on the eleventh hole Professional **Pete** sneezed violently just as he hit the **ball** and it shot straight off the tee and into the **rough**. **Sid** was so shocked he almost fainted and fell over. Professional **Pete** went straight after the **ball**, he wasn't quite sure hot find a lost **golf ball** as he'd never had to do it before, but he waded into the **rough** and hacked about with his club for a while.

After five minutes **Sid** said, "Perhaps you'd better give up on this hole."
But **Pete** said, "Can't do that."
After ten minutes **Sid** said, "Look it's only a **golf ball** and it's about time I won a hole. Give in."
But **Pete** said, "No way."

After half an hour **Sid** said, "I'm getting hungry."
But **Pete** said, "This is my favourite **ball**, I can't abandon it."
After three hours **Sid** said, "Bye!"
And **Pete** said, "You go **Sid**, I've got to stay here till I find that **ball**."
As he went **Sid** said, "But you've got nine others, and if you stay here you'll end up losing the whole game and I'll win!"

And that's how Professional **Pete** lost his first game in ten years.
"This **ball** may be little but it's too important to lose, it doesn't matter how many others I've got, I've never lost a **golf ball** before and I won't lose one now."
And twelve hours later, as the moon shone down at midnight, **Pete** bent down and found his lost **golf ball**. He smiled to himself, put it safely in his bag and went off home to celebrate. He'd lost the game but found the **ball**.

The Parable of the Fishing Net

Net – Mime throwing a large net out to sea
Fish – All open and close mouths like goldfish, making *puh* sound
Conkers – Mime playing conkers, swinging one at another
Mail – "Post!"
Ticking – Say "Tick" three times
Complaining – "Rhubarb, rhubarb, rhubarb"
Tea – "Sluuuuuuurp"

Jesus once told a story about a fisherman who threw his **net** into the sea then pulled it out and found it was full of **fish**. So the man sat down next to the **net** and sorted out all the good **fish** from all the **bad** fish. That is, he separated all the **fish** he could eat from all the **fish** he couldn't eat.

Nowadays Jesus might tell a story about a man going out for a walk in the autumn leaves, picking up a huge pile of **conkers** and then going home and sorting out all the good strong **conkers** from all the bad rotten **conkers**.

Or, it's like a woman going downstairs in the morning and collecting the **mail** from her front doormat. Then she makes a cup of **tea** and sits down and sorts out all the junk **mail** from the rest of the **mail**. And she throws the junk **mail** in the bin.

Whether it's **fish**, **conkers**, or **mail**, it's similar to what will happen when history comes to an end, when the clock of time stops **ticking**. Then God will collect everyone together and separate those who want to be with him from those who don't want to be with him. And there will be a lot of **complaining**, but by then it will be too late, the clock of time will have stopped **ticking**.

Good Sam

Posh businessman - "Oh, I say"
Bus stop/Bus - "Ding! Ding!"
Dirty - "Phaw!"
Churchwarden - Shake hands with the person next to you
When narrator places hand to ear shout - "Good Sam the tramp"
Football supporters - Half audience shout for one team, half shout for another

Once, there was a **bus stop**. And there were three people waiting at this **bus stop**. First, there was a **posh businessman**, who had a very big house, and lots of money.

Then there was the local **churchwarden**. He had a house, and quite a lot of money, but not as much as the **posh businessman**. The third person at the bus stop was called... (**Hand to ear**)

He was a very **dirty** tramp because he didn't have a house, or any money; he lived in a cardboard box. And he didn't have any friends - because he was so **dirty**.

Well, just then, a gang of **football supporters** went running past the **bus stop**. And these **football supporters** made a lot of noise. They didn't notice the **posh businessman**, the **churchwarden** or (**Hand to ear**) - but they did see the schoolteacher coming the other way. And as they got to the **bus stop**, the **football supporters** grabbed him, threw him to the ground, and stole his wallet, his watch and all his money. Then they ran off, leaving him lying on the ground.

Just then, the **bus** arrived. The **posh businessman** looked at the teacher, then quickly jumped on the **bus** - because he couldn't stand the sight of blood.

The **churchwarden** - well, he looked at the teacher, then he saw the **businessman** jump on the **bus**, and he decided to do the same, because he was frightened of **football supporters**.

Meanwhile... (**Hand to ear**) who was standing on the end, he saw the teacher, and he felt sorry for him. So he missed the **bus**, went over to the man, and helped him up. Then he gave the teacher 50p, which was all the money he'd got from begging. And even though Sam was very **dirty**, the teacher didn't mind, because... he took him to a hospital and made sure that he was okay.

Now, which person was a neighbour to the teacher? Not the **posh businessman**, nor the **churchwarden** - no, the man's neighbour was... (**Hand to ear**) because he showed him love, he acted like a friend.

Zacchaeus

Tree – "Rustle, rustle"   **Money** – "Chink, chink"
Tea – "Munch, munch"   **Little** - Crouch down
Taxes/Tax Collector – "Sssss!"

Once there was a man called Zacchaeus. He was a very **little** man and he couldn't see very much because everyone else was always taller. No one liked him because he was a **tax collector**. Every day he used to sit under his favourite **tree** collecting **taxes** off the people, but he used to force them to pay more **money** than they need to, so he could keep some for himself. In those days **tax collectors** weren't very nice people.

Now one day a huge crowd of people gathered in the street because there was a special person coming to town and while Zacchaeus was counting his **money** under his **tree** he was suddenly surrounded. Well, he couldn't see a thing because he was too little so he jumped up into his favourite **tree** and there on the road he saw a man. Well, everyone could see him sitting up in the **tree** and suddenly this man looked up at him and called out:
"Hey, Zacchaeus, come down from that **tree**!"
"Why?" he said, "I've only just got up here."
"Because I'm coming to your house for some **tea**."
"Some **tea**?"
"Yes," said the man, "because I want to get to know you."

Well, the man's name was Jesus, and while he and Zacchaeus had some **tea** they became good friends and Zacchaeus realised that he shouldn't have taken all that **money** from the people.
"I know!" he said, "I'll give away twice as much as I've taken from people." (**Encourage everyone to cheer**)
"No I won't. (**All say: "Aaaah"**) I'll give away three times as much. (**Cheer**)
No I won't… (**"Aaaah"**) I'll give away four times as much!"   (**Cheer**)
And that's exactly what he did and from then on Zacchaeus and Jesus were really good friends.

The Shopping Trip

by Soobie Whitfield

Shopping - Checkout noise "Beep,beep!" and appropriate action
Food of any kind - "Yum, Yum!"
Children - All children cheer
Lost - "OH NO!!" Hands up to face
Said - "Stay together, hold tight. Don't fuss, don't fight."

One Saturday Mrs Brown decided to go **shopping**. **Shopping** was always an adventure for Mrs Brown because she had seven **children** - Jimmy, Johnny, Timmy, Tommy, Susie, Sally and Eric. So they got their **shopping** bags and set out for Tesco's. The place was packed solid so Mrs Brown called all the **children** to her and **said**: "Stay together, hold tight, don't fuss, don't fight." Then she took out her **shopping** list and asked the children to help. She sent Jimmy, Johnny and Timmy to the freezers to fetch **fish fingers** and **beef burgers**. As they went she **said**: "..." and so off they went. She sent Tommy and Suzie to the bread counter to get a large white sliced **loaf** and a **fruitcake** for Sunday. As they disappeared round the corner she warned them not to get lost. Finally she asked Sally and Eric to get a box of **cornflakes**.

On their way Eric spotted some **chocolate** piled high on the shelves. He was just wandering off to get a closer look when Sally **said**: "..." Eric shouted back: "I'll only be a minute," and disappeared round the corner. Back at the checkout Mrs Brown and the **children** were unloading a very full trolley. Down the conveyor belt went all the food. Mrs Brown lifted the heavy **shopping** bags into the trolley, and started to walk towards the car park. As she moved away she looked over her shoulder and **said**: "..." "STOP!!" shouted Sally, "We've **lost** Eric." Mrs Brown left her **shopping** and started to search Tesco's for her missing son. She went to the **cornflake** shelf, the **bread** counter, the freezers and the **cake** stand. But she couldn't find him - he was definitely **lost**. So she asked the shop assistant to help her look. Soon Tesco's was full of people looking for **lost** Eric.

Just then Mrs Brown walked round a corner - and there was Eric! She took his hand and when the **children** saw him coming they shouted: "Where have you been? We were worried. We **lost** you."

But Mrs Brown just smiled. She picked Eric up in her arms and hugged him.

"I'm very happy," she told him, "you were **lost** but now you're back and we're all together again."

Lots of Miracle Men

Caesar – All bow
Pretending – Give a sly wink
Messengers – Place hands to mouth and shout "Listen!"
Trick – Snigger behind hands

In the days when Jesus was on the earth, walking about, making friends, meeting people and telling them all about God, there were lots of other people walking around, **pretending** to be important. **Pretending** to be special. **Pretending** to be miracle men. **Pretending** to be **messengers** from God.

Now the Pharisees, who were like priests and ministers back then, they went around asking these people difficult questions to find out if they were really God's **messengers**, or if they were just **pretending**.

When they saw a man preaching on a street corner they might go up to him and ask a question like this:

"Should we pay taxes to **Caesar** or not?"

And if the man said: "Yes." they would not listen to him, because they didn't like **Caesar**.

And if the man said "No." then they would sneak off to **Caesar** and the Romans and tell them to arrest the man.

And if the answer were "I don't know." then they'd just laugh at the person for **pretending** to be a messenger from God.

You see, they didn't really want to know the answer; they just wanted to **trick** people.

So, one day they went up to Jesus and asked him:

"Should we pay taxes to **Caesar** or not?"

Now Jesus was very clever and he knew they were just trying to **trick** him, like they **tricked** everyone else. So Jesus asked them for some money. He held it up and said:

"Whose picture is stamped on this money?"

The Pharisees looked at the money and said, "**Caesar's** of course."

So Jesus replied, "Well then, pay **Caesar** what belongs to **Caesar** and pay God what belongs to him."

The Pharisees looked puzzled and didn't know what to say to that. They were well and truly stumped.

"Drat!" they muttered, "We'll have to think of a new question for **tricking** people with now."

And some of them realised that Jesus wasn't **pretending**, he really was a **messenger** from God, and one or two of them even began to realise the truth, he wasn't just a **messenger**... He was God's very own son.

Doing Their Best

Coke - Mime opening can, say "Fizzzz!"
Trip - "Oops!"
Best - Punch the air and say "Yea!"
Assistants – "Yes sir!"
Trampolines – "Boiing!"
Swimming pool – "Splosh!"

There was once a man who owned a leisure centre. It was the best leisure centre around, and it was run by the man's three **assistants**: Dirk, Digby and Dougal. One day the man decided to go on a **trip** around the world. So he called in the three **assistants** and said to them:
"I'm going on a **trip** around the world - and I want you to look after my leisure centre for me."
First - he put Dirk in charge of the **swimming pool**. Then he put Digby in charge of the **trampolines**, the table tennis and the **coke** machines. Dougal was put in the toilets - to look after them.
Then the owner told them to do their **best** and he waved goodbye and left on his **trip**.

It took Dirk 10 seconds to decide what to do.
It took Digby 10 minutes to decide what to do.
It took Dougal 10 days to decide what to do - but he got there in the end!

Three weeks later the owner returned.
"Hello!" he said to his **assistants**, "I had a nice **trip**. Now - what have you been doing with my leisure centre?"
Dirk jumped up and said: "I cleaned the **swimming pool** every day, put in a brand new inflatable shark, rescued three people in difficulties and I made £500 profit."
"Well done," said the owner.
Dougal jumped forward and said: "I cleaned the toilets every day, put in some brand new fluorescent toilet paper and some delicious chocolate soap, and I charged everyone 20p a minute to go in. Here's the profit: £200."

The owner was very pleased when he saw they had done their best. Then he turned to Digby.

Digby said: "I locked up the **trampolines** so the children couldn't get at them, then I sat on the table tennis table and drank all the **coke** - it was very tasty."

"What?" said the owner, "You mean you wasted all that time and money - was that all you could do?"

"Well, I think you work people too hard," said Digby, "and I felt like having a rest, and anyway - I wanted to look after the **swimming pool** - not the **trampolines**."

The owner was so angry with him that he gave Digby the sack and threw him outside. But he promoted his other two **assistants** and he gave them both a pay rise because he knew he could trust them to always do their **best**.

The Widow's Mite (2)

Rich - Rub fingers and say "Money, money, money, money"
Poor – Mime pulling a tiny coin out of your pocket and
hold it up between finger and thumb
Servants – Bow   **Talking** - "Rabbit, rabbit!"
Box - "Rattle Clink!"   **Whistle** - All whistle

This story is about two people, one who was **rich** and one who was poor.
The **rich** person was a man who had a big house and lots of **servants**. One
day he decided to go to church to put some money into the collection **box**.
So he called his **servants**, told them to bring three large bags of gold coins,
and they all set off talking together.
The **rich** man was very happy that day and he started to **whistle** as he
walked along. The **servants** weren't quite so happy because the money
bags were heavy but they **whistled** as well, because the **rich** man told them
to.

As they got near the church they saw a crowd of people **talking**. The **rich**
man carried on **whistling** and went over to them. They were all **talking** to
Jesus, but the **rich** man wasn't really interested so he took his **servants** into
the church. Inside there was a large, wooden collection **box**. The **servants**
had a rest while the man picked up the first bag, and one by one he put the
gold coins into the **box**. When the bag was empty he picked up the second
one and put more coins into the **box**. He enjoyed doing this and **whistled**
loudly. After he had put the third bag into the **box** they all got up and went
outside. On their way out they bumped into a **poor** widow, she was very,
very, very **poor** - but the **rich** man hardly saw her and he and his **servants**
happily walked home.

The **poor** widow crept quietly to the **box** and put in two small pennies. It
was all she had and it only took two seconds to do it, then she quickly ran
outside again. But Jesus had been watching everything, and he turned to all
the people who were **talking**, and he said to them:
"That **poor** widow put a lot more in the **box** than the **rich** man did -
because she put in everything that she had."

Lazarus

Amazed - Open mouth and eyes as wide as possible
Waited - Drum fingers impatiently
Footstep - Make the sound of a single step
Meal - Mime holing up a plate and smelling food
Talk - Place hand to ear, to listen
Worse - Shake head sadly

Once there was a man who didn't feel very well.

He had two sisters and they started to worry about him.

One of the sisters, Martha, made him his favourite **meal** to help him feel better, but he didn't eat any of it.

So his other sister, Mary, went and sat next to him so they could have a good **talk** and she could cheer him up. But Lazarus didn't say very much. He was not well at all and he was getting **worse**.

So one of the sister's had an idea.

"Let's ask his best friend to come and see him," said Mary. "That'll help."

"Good idea," said Martha, "I'll find out where he is."

So they looked around and asked a few people and they found out that their Lazarus's friend was a long way away in another town.

"Oh dear," said Mary. "What can we do? We gave him a **meal** and we tried to **talk** but nothing helped."

"I know," said Mary, "let's send someone to go and find his friend. When he hears about Lazarus he'll come and help."

So they sent someone with a message. Then they **waited**. And they **waited**. And they **waited**.

In the meantime their brother got **worse** and **worse** and **worse,** and in the end poor Lazarus got so ill that he died. Mary and Martha were heart-broken and they had a special service for Lazarus and they buried him in a cave.

Then there was a **footstep** outside and a knock at the door. Martha went to answer it. It was Lazarus's best friend. It was Jesus.

"Where've you been?" yelled Martha. "It's too late. Our brother's dead. Where've you been? We **waited** for you... if you'd been here he wouldn't have died, but it's too late now."

Jesus was very upset when he saw what had happened to his friend Lazarus. He sat down and cried. Martha told Mary that Jesus had come and Mary ran out to see him. Jesus went with them to the cave where Lazarus was buried.

Jesus stood outside and said, "Open the cave."

Martha looked **amazed**. "But Lazarus is in there and he's been dead for four days. It'll smell terrible."

"Open the cave," said Jesus.

So they rolled the stone back from the entrance to the cave, and Jesus looked up to heaven, said a prayer and then shouted,

"Lazarus! Come out!"

Everyone stood watching, **amazed**.

"Lazarus! Come out!" said Jesus.

There was a tense, silent moment, and then they heard a **footstep**. And another, and another, and another. And then Lazarus appeared, still wrapped from head to foot in grave clothes. But he was alive and well. Jesus smiled and said, "Unwrap and let him go!"

And once again the people were **amazed**.

The Triumphal Entry

by Keith Fraser-Smith

Followers - Tramp/tramp movement and sound with feet
Riding/Rode - Riding movements
Donkey - "Eaw, eaw!"
Crowd/s - Cheer: "Hooray! Hooray!"
Hosanna - Pretend to wave flags
Booed – All shout "Boo!"

It was the last visit Jesus would make to Jerusalem. He told two of his **followers** to go and pick up transport from *Peter's Rent a Donkey*. Jesus got up onto the donkey and **rode** it into the city. His **followers** followed him. When he got close to Jerusalem a big **crowd** began to gather. Some people in the **crowd** cut down palm branches and threw them in the road in front of the **donkey** that Jesus was **riding**. They took off their coats too and threw them in front of the **donkey**. Then they started shouting "**Hosanna** to the Don of David, blessed is he who comes in the name of the Lord. **Hosanna** in the highest."
The **donkey** kept walking. Jesus kept **riding**. They weren't afraid of the **crowds**. They kept on shouting: "**Hosanna**!"

And so Jesus came into Jerusalem **riding** on a **donkey**, followed by his **followers**, and cheered on by the **crowds**.
Jesus was very popular but later that week it would all change - there would be no **donkey**, his **followers** would run away, (Tramp feet very fast) and the **crowds** - no they **booed** him. Jesus became the most unpopular person in Jerusalem and a terrible thing happened to him. He was put to death by being nailed on a wooden cross.

Palm Sunday Crowd Story

Suitable for an outdoor or large event, the responses are fairly noisy, like those in a pantomime. Similar in style to the *Christmas Crowd Story*.

"...can't do that!" - Divide the crowd in two for this response:
1. "Oh yes you can," 2. "Oh no you can't."
Donkey – All shout: "Which donkey?"
Grumble/Grumbling - Divide the crowd into 4 groups and say in sequence: 1. "Mumble, mumble!" 2. "Rhubarb, rhubarb!"
3. "Leave it out!" 4. "You're having a laugh!"

Picture the scene: Jesus and his followers have been travelling for a long time and they're worn out. So Jesus gets his disciples together and says: "Listen mates, I think it's time for the **donkey**. The one you're gonna get from that town over there."
"Hang on guv." said the disciples, "we can't just walk in and pinch one - we **can't do that**!"
So Jesus sat them all down and said:
"Now, look, I've had this plan worked out for a while. Two of you are gonna nip into the town, and when you see the **donkey**... The one in the town! It'll be next to another **donkey**... The one with the other **donkey**... oh don't worry - you'll know it when you see it!"
Now the disciples weren't so sure and they started having a **grumble**.
"Look it's no use **grumbling**." said Jesus, "It's all worked out, you two nip in there and bring back the first **donkey** you see. Don't start that again! If you get any bother just say: The master needs it."

So they nipped off into the town, and sure enough they saw the two... animals tied up. So one of them kept watch while the other untied them. Suddenly two massive bruisers appeared, looking very mean. One of them shouted: "Hey! You **can't do that**!"
"No you can't," said the men, "'cause that's our **donkey**!" Now this confused the two big men, so the disciples quickly chipped in: "The master needs it!" And off they went, leaving the two bruisers standing there, **grumbling**.

As soon as they got back Jesus got on the **donkey**. Er... the one on the left, and he rode into Jerusalem in front of huge crowds of people, all shouting and singing and praising God. Well... most of the people had a great time, but a few of them - the priests and religious leaders - all they could do was **grumble**. But nobody cared, because all they wanted to do was see Jesus - for he was the King.

Communion Rap

Bread – Sniff as if smelling fresh bread
Wine – Mime holding up a cup of wine
Table – Knock on something wooden   **Soon** – Check watch on wrist
See – Look amazed and shocked   **Respect** – Give each other five
Meal – Make eating sounds   **Broke/Broken** - Mime breaking a bread roll

On the night before Friday, not a moment too **soon**
Jesus took his friends to an upper room.
They had a good **meal** and a real nice chat
And this is what happened right after that.

There was a hunk of **bread** on the **table** there
So Jesus picked it up and he said a prayer
Then he **broke** it in pieces and he said to them
Take it and eat it 'cause I'm your friend.

There was a cup of **wine** on the **table** too
So he lifted that up and he said "Thank you."
Then he passed it round, the **wine** was red
And when they'd all had a drink this is what he said:

"This **wine** is like the blood pumping round my heart
And it's going to be the sign of a brand new start,
My body will be **broken**, just like this **bread**
And my blood will be spilled and I will be dead.

You'll **see** it happen before your very eyes
But three days later you'll **see** me rise.
Death won't hold me - I'll break the chains
And **soon** I promise I'll be back again.

And when you meet together from time to time
Remember me with **bread** and **wine**
This **bread** is my body and my blood is this **wine**.
And if you take it with **respect** then you'll be fine."

Good Friday

History - Open hands like a book and blow dust
Prison - "Clang!" and clap hands together
Run away - Turn away and put hands up, rejecting
Numbers 1 to 10 - Hold up same number of fingers

It felt like the longest day in **history**.
Jesus had been arrested and was taken to **prison**.
Everybody had turned against him and his friends had **run away**.

Jesus had to go through 10 horrible experiences all on his own.

1   They took Jesus to the priest's house. There they asked him lots of
       questions and told lies about him.

2   The soldiers took him outside, hit him and spat in his face.

3   They took Jesus to Pontius Pilate - the man in charge of executions.
       There they accused him of saying things against God.

4   They took him to Herod the king. Herod made Jesus wear a purple
       robe, laughed at him and made fun of him.

5   They sent him back to Pontius Pilate and he had Jesus whipped by
       the soldiers. The soldiers also made a crown out of long thorns and
       they pressed it onto Jesus' head.

6   They took Jesus out to a large crowd of people who all wanted
       Jesus to be crucified. So they set a guilty man free and decided to
       kill Jesus in his place.

7   The soldiers made Jesus carry a huge wooden cross up a long hill to
       a place called Golgotha. The cross was so heavy that he fell down
       on the way.

8   They nailed Jesus to the cross and crucified him in front of all the people. The crowds laughed, shouted and jeered at him.

9   The soldiers stole his clothes and played games to decide who would have his coat.

10   After many painful hours on the cross Jesus prayed for all the people and then - he died.

It felt like the longest day in **history**.
Jesus was arrested and taken to **prison**.
Everybody turned against him and his friends had **run away**.

He had never done anything wrong, never hurt anyone, never stolen anything, never even told a lie.
But the people killed him - as if he was guilty.
He died in our place.

He died for you and me.

The Commission

[Also appropriate for Ascension Day]

Hill – Pant and huff
Walk/Walked - Make walking steps on the spot
Gift - "It's for you!"   **Leave -** Wave, say "Bye!"
Answer to any question – No   **Up –** Look up sharply

Our story starts quite a few days after Jesus had risen from the dead. He called all his disciples together and took them for a **walk**. They started going **up** a **hill** together.
While they **walked** Jesus told them that God had a very special **gift** for them, to help them live their lives. But first he had to leave them. They wondered where he might go. **On holiday?** No. **On a ship?** No. **On a journey?** No.

So as they **walked** to the top of this **hill** Jesus told them about the **gift**. He was going to **leave** so that they could have this **gift**. The disciples wondered what it might be. **Was it some food? Or a game? Or a car?** Jesus said the **gift** was the Holy Spirit. He told the disciples to go all over the world telling people about God, praying for them and doing miracles.

Well, they were all tired now from the **walk** and the disciples didn't feel like doing any miracles right at that moment. They wanted to sit down on the **hill**. At the top of the **hill** Jesus told them they had to wait for the gift in Jerusalem, and then he said goodbye to them all. The disciples were very sad because they didn't want Jesus to **leave**. But he stood on the **hill** and suddenly began to go **up** in the air. **Was he flying?** He was being lifted **up** to heaven by God.

The disciples were amazed and stayed on the **hill** a long time, looking **up**, and thinking about Jesus **leaving**. Then two men in white appeared and said, "Why are still standing here looking **up**? You've seen Jesus **leave** – but he will be back one day." So the disciples turned away and **walked** back down the **hill**, back home to wait for the **gift** that Jesus had promised. The **gift** of the Holy Spirit.

The Day of Pentecost

Frightened - "HELP!"
Fire - "Crackle, crackle" and waggle fingers like flames
Wind - Whistling sounds
Jesus - Cheer
Language - "Jibber jabber" Nod head side to side as you say this

It all began a few days after **Jesus** had gone back up to heaven. The disciples were feeling very sad and **frightened**. They met together every day to talk about things, but no one really knew what to do. **Jesus** had been their friend and their guide and now they felt lost and **frightened** without him. Peter tried hard to encourage them but they all felt very alone and very **frightened**.

On one particular day they were all together in one room praying and sitting quietly when all of a sudden it felt like there was a strong **wind** blowing. Peter ran to the window and looked out - but it was all peaceful outside - the **wind** was blowing in the house!
Then a **fire** appeared floating in the air in the middle of the room, and little flames came out of the **fire** and touched each person. But no one got burnt because the **fire** and the rushing **wind** were from **Jesus** and it meant they were being filled with God's Spirit, and instead of feeling **frightened** they started to feel fantastic.

Then the **wind** and the **fire** stopped and they began to talk in lots of different **languages**, as God gave them each a new **language** to speak. So, as they chattered away they walked outside where there were lots of people from all different countries. And suddenly they realised - these **languages** they were speaking were the same as the **languages** of all these different countries. So they told them all about **Jesus**, and more than three thousand people decided to become Christians that day. And that was the start of the church.

Saul and the Bright Light

Bodyguard –Flex muscles
Light – Shield eyes and look up
Voice – Place hand to ear
Straight – Shoot arm out straight
Fright – Look very scared

There was a man called Saul, who wasn't very tall, and he didn't like Christian folk.
He'd give you a **fright** if you'd seen the **light** and it really was no joke.

One day he said, "Let's go to Damascus instead," and he climbed aboard his horse.
He rode off hard, with a big **bodyguard**, but something changed his course.

They'd not gone far when something bizarre gave them all a **fright**,
The horses stopped and the **bodyguard** dropped as the sky grew very bright.

"Who are you, Lord?" said trembling Saul, "What's this **light** above?"
"I am Jesus," said the **voice**, "And I thought I'd give you a shove."

"When you go round putting Christians down, it's me you're really after."
And the **voice** went on, clear and strong, "Saul, you couldn't be dafter."

"You may think it odd, but you can't beat God. So get up and listen, mate.
Go **straight** into the city and **straight** to a street called **Straight**."

When Paul got up, he was all shook up; his face was scared and white.
His **bodyguard** was shaking too; they'd all had quite a **fright**.

Saul looked around but there was no sound, all was dark and grim.
He said, "I can't see, a thing." The **light** had blinded him.

In a street called **Straight** they met a mate, Judas he was called.
They stayed with him till a man popped looking for brother Saul.

The man came to call to pray for Saul that he might see the **light**
To Saul's surprise scales fell of his eyes and he could see all right.

And soon brother Saul became St Paul now he'd seen the **light**.
And he did his best to tell all the rest about his new friend Jesus Christ.

Paul's Narrow Escape

Stop - Hold up hands like a traffic cop   **Basket** – "Creak!"
Bananas – All pull funny faces   **Argument** – All shout "Quiet!"
Plan – Mime holding a bit of paper and turn it round one
way then the other, trying to read it   **Gates** – "Squeak… Clang!"

Paul was a very enthusiastic man. Before he was a Christian he tried very hard to **stop** the Christians, as soon as he became a Christian he tried very hard to **stop** the non-Christians!
You might say that whatever he did Paul put his back into it.

So, as soon as Paul met God on the road to Damascus he decided it was time to convert every single person he met. He started by going into the synagogue where all the Jewish priests and religious teachers were and he told them they'd got it all wrong and needed to **stop** and think again. Oh dear!

They went **bananas**. All the priests and the religious teachers couldn't work out what had happened. They said, "Wait a minute! **Stop**! Isn't this the same man who wanted to kill all the Christians? What's he doing trying to convert us then? He must be **bananas**!"

This went on for a few days and Paul's preaching was so good that soon they all had a big **argument**, and after the big **argument** they decided that the best thing to do was to kill Paul. So they got together and made up a **plan**. Every night they would secretly watch the **gates** of the city waiting for Paul to leave so they could pounce on him and catch him. But Paul found out about their **plan** and even though they watched the **gates** every night, they didn't catch him.

Instead, Paul's friends came up with their own **plan**, late one night they tied a rope to a large **basket**, and then they climbed up onto the wall far away from the city **gates**, and they put Paul inside the **basket** and lowered him down to safety. Then Paul ran away from the city and went out into the desert and lived there for a while.

Peter and Cornelius

Cornelius – All sit up straight to attention
Simon/s – "Who?"   **Snakes** – All hiss
Reptiles – Poke out slithery tongues like lizards
Birds – "Flap! Flap!"   **Eat** – Make loud chomping sounds

Once upon a time there was a very important man called **Cornelius**, he was a good man, and a Captain in the Roman army.
He did a lot to help the poor people, and he and his family prayed and worshipped God.

One day at three o'clock in the afternoon **Cornelius** decided to spend some time praying, so he went into his house and closed the door.
He'd only just started saying his prayers when suddenly he heard a noise.
He opened his and saw a man in shining clothes standing in front of him.
Cornelius looked astonished.
"Who are you?" he stammered.
"**Cornelius**, God's sent me to have a word with you… Now listen, here's the plan. God has heard your prayers and he knows that you are a very kind man. So, he wants you to go to a place called Joppa and find a man called **Simon**, he's staying in a house with another man also called **Simon**."
"Two **Simons**?"
"Yes, they're both called **Simon**."
"How do I know the difference?"
"Yes, one's called **Simon** the tanner, the other's called **Simon** Peter."
"Which one do I need?"
"**Simon** Peter –
So **Cornelius** called a couple of his servants and another soldier and told them to go and look for **Simon** the tanner and **Simon** Peter. And they set off.

The next day, at the house of **Simon** the tanner, **Simon** Peter decided to go up onto the roof to pray. As he was talking to God a blanket suddenly fell out of the sky and made him jump. When he looked at it he saw that there were all kinds of **snakes** and **reptiles** and **birds** on it.

Then another blanket fell out of the sky and that had **snakes** and **reptiles** and **birds** on it. Peter said, "Ugh!" but he heard a voice say, "Don't say ugh! Why not **eat** them instead?"

Peter was very confused by this, then another blanket fell out of the sky, and this one was full of **snakes** and **reptiles** and **birds** too, they seemed to be all around him now, creeping and crawling and squawking. And the voice said, "Here's some more, you can **eat** these too."

But Peter said, "We're not supposed to **eat** these kinds of animals."

And the voice said, "Don't say that, I decide what is okay and what is not okay."

Just then Peter heard a shout outside. He went downstairs and saw some men standing at the gate.

They asked him "Are you called **Simon**?"

"Yes," he said. "I'm also called Peter."

The men stayed for a night, and the very next day they took Peter to see **Cornelius**.

When they met Peter said, "I think God was telling me about you, I saw a lot of **snakes** and **reptiles** and **birds**… And God told me to **eat** them, though we're not supposed to. I think he was telling me that it's time for people who aren't Jews to get to know God. You see, at the moment all the people who are followers are Jews and we always thought that it was only for Jews, but it's not is it, you're a good man **Cornelius**, you are already getting to know God and now he's sent me here to help you."

The Prison Breakout

Dragged – Pull at your own collar, as if dragging yourself away
Wow! – "Wow!"
Prison – Mime turning a key in a lock and say "Click Clunk!"
Shake/Shook – All tremble
Bad guys – All say "Gurrr!" and look mean

Some people are sent to **prison** because they have done something wrong, like stealing, or spying or smashing things up.

But sometimes people are sent to **prison** because of the things they believe. Like Paul and Silas.

They were arrested one day for helping a fortuneteller. She made a lot of money by predicting the future, and when she Met Paul and Silas she could see immediately that they were servants and friends of God. So Paul prayed for her and set her free from the evil spirit that made her predict the future. The woman felt a lot better but the men who made money out of her were not happy at all, they grabbed hold of Paul and Silas and **dragged** them into the town square. They told the officials in charge of the city that Paul and Silas were causing trouble and should be punished so the officials grabbed them, and ordered them to be whipped. It hurt a lot and Paul and Silas were injured badly. Then the officials **dragged** them into **prison**, but Paul and Silas didn't give up, instead they sang songs to God in the **prison**.

Just around midnight there was a loud rumbling sound and the ground began to **shake** and **shake** and **shake**.

The jailer ran in and cried, "What's going on?"

Just then there was a very big earthquake, so big that it **shook** the doors off the prison, and there was nothing to stop the prisoners from escaping and running away.

"Oh no!" said the jailer, and he **shook** with terror, "this is terrible, I've let all the **bad guys** out. It's all my fault."

Of course it wasn't really his fault but he felt so bad about it that he picked up a sword and got ready to kill himself.

Then he a heard a voice yell, "**Wow!** Stop! Wait a minute!"

The jailer picked up a torch and looked into the **prison**, all the **bad guys** were still there, and Paul and Silas were there too.

"We're still here," said Paul, "it's okay, don't hurt yourself."

The jailer was amazed, he'd heard about Paul and Silas and knew they believed in God.

"Tell me about this God of yours," said the jailer, "I want to know how to be saved by him."

So Paul and Silas started to tell him, but he said, "**Wow**! Stop! Wait a minute!"

And he **dragged** them over to his house.

"Tell all my family about him too!" he said.

And so that night Paul and Silas told the jailer and all his family about God and every one of them believed in God and decided to follow him.

Putting on the Armour

First, second, third etc. – Hold up appropriate number of fingers and shout number aloud, e.g. **First** – Shout "One" and hold up one finger
Belt – Mime doing up a strong belt
Armour – Slap hands on stomach or chest
Shoes – Mime pulling shoes
Shield – Mime holding up a shield and dodge around behind it
Helmet – Pretend to pull on a helmet
Sword – Pretend to hold up a large sword

When a Roman soldier used to go into battle he first put on special armour for protection.

First he put on a good strong **belt** over his leather tunic.
Second he put on a plate of **armour** across his chest.
Third he put on **shoes** for marching and running.
Fourth he carried a big **shield** to protect himself from the enemy.
Fifth He put on his metal **helmet**.
Sixth he picked up his **sword** for fighting the battle.

Now, in God's armour the **belt** we can put around our waist is truth, we can try to be honest and open.
The **armour** on our chest is the new life we have, forgiven and accepted and changed by God.
For our **shoes** we have a desire to tell other people about Jesus, that's what keeps us on the move.
Our **shield** is our trust in God, he will protect us like he protected David against Goliath the giant.
Next - the **helmet**. We have been rescued by God, he sent Jesus to come and save us from the bad things and that's like wearing a **helmet** to keep us safe from being hurt.
And the Bible is like a **sword** – we don't hit people with it, but we can tell people what's inside it and that will help us through each day and help us fight our way through the problems we might face.

So **first**: the **belt** of truth.
Second: the **armour** of being right with God.
Third: the **shoes** of telling other people about Jesus.
Fourth: the big **shield** of our trust in God.
Fifth: the **helmet** of being rescued.
And **sixth**: the **sword** of the Bible for fighting the battle.

And **seventh**: we can talk to God about everything we do and everyone we know. And that's the last weapon we have on top of… (Say this list quickly) the **belt**, the **armour**, the **shoes**, the **shield**, the **helmet**, the **sword** – the weapon of praying.
So one more time: the **belt**, the **armour**, the **shoes**, the **shield**, the **helmet**, the **sword** and… the weapon of praying.
Amen!

John's Big Screen Adventure

Heaven – Smooth hands across the imaginary sky above your head
Screen – Look up, and mime chewing popcorn
World – Mime holding a big globe
Amazing – Open eyes and mouth wide and look suitably amazed
Thunder – Cover ears and make a loud rumbling sound
Horse/s – Make sound of galloping hooves
Hail – "Rat-a -tat-tat!"

John had been a close friend of Jesus, in fact, one of his best friends. When he was much older, years and years after Jesus was taken up to heaven John was arrested for telling people about his friend Jesus, but instead of being put in prison he was put on an island called Patmos.
One Sunday as he was standing outside looking up towards **heaven** suddenly the skies above him filled with an amazing moving picture. The clouds turned into a big dazzling white cinema **screen** and as he watched an amazing film began show on it, a film about the future, about the **world** and about God. As he watched the **screen** turned a golden colour and a man appeared on it, a man with shimmering snow-white hair, fiery red eyes, a voice like **thunder** and with his hands full of shooting stars. When John saw him he was so amazed he fell down. Then a movie soundtrack began to play and John heard the words,
"Don't be frightened, I am the one who died and came back to life. I was here at the beginning of the **world**, and I'll be here at the end of it. Now watch all these things I show you and write down what you see."

The man faded out of the shot and a massive golden door appeared on the **screen**, shining and shimmering, it swung open all on its own and suddenly John could see right inside **heaven**. It was quite **amazing**. John could see a throne room and there was huge throne in it, covered in diamonds and emeralds and precious stones. It sparkled and shone. Lightning suddenly shot out from it like streaks of jagged flames of fire and **thunder** rumbled and clapped so loud that it made John jump. Prowling around the throne were four strange animals. They were covered in eyes and could see absolutely everywhere.

John could see a man sitting on the golden throne, he picked up a large scroll and held onto it for a long time, then when he opened it John heard the sound of galloping hooves and from nowhere a huge white **horse** came riding across the **screen** then a fiery red **horse** appeared and came chasing after the white one. Then a jet-black **horse** came racing across the **screen** and finally a deathly pale **horse** galloped across. Then a door opened and seven men stepped into the throne room, they were tall and bright, in yellow tunics, and they were all carrying trumpets. They each gave a blast on their trumpet and **hail** and fire came pouring out of the sky, then the stars and the moon and the sun began to change colour and burn up. Then the scene changed to the sea and the water was red and full of boats all crashing and sinking in the fire and **hail**.

Then there was a loud roar and the sea turned all foamy and suddenly a huge monster rose up out of the water, swallowing up all the ships in the sea. It swam through the fire and **hail** to the beach and began walking out of the water, it was huge like a dinosaur and it started eating everything in its way and crushing tower blocks with its tail.   Then suddenly the white **horse** appeared on the beach, followed by a whole army of white **horses** and riders and the monster turned to attack them and they had a big battle that went on and on and on, until, at last the monster fell onto the sand defeated. Then the **horses** and riders threw a huge net over and they dragged it far along the beach and on through towns and villages until they came to a huge foaming red lake. And they threw the monster into the lake where he drowned and disappeared.

At the end of the adventure, when the **screen** in the sky had faded away, and the sights of **heaven** and the sounds of **thunder** had disappeared John sat back against a tree and scribbled down the **amazing** things he'd seen about the **world** and **heaven,** about the monster and the **horses,** and he thought about it all for a long, long time.

This Ol' Earth

Get the audience to click their fingers as you rap the following reading, and ask them to repeat the last line of each verse twice. You may like to run through these at the beginning.

Some drop litter; leave graffiti on a seat.
Some trash bottles, leaving glass out on the street.
It ain't just a mess it's about self-worth
And it's all about the way we treat the good ol' earth.

All: And it's all about the way we treat the good ol' earth. x2

All of us are crazy we waste so much
All of us are lazy and out of touch.
We don't realise the mountain of things
That ends up sitting in our own waste bins.

All: That ends up sitting in our own waste bins. x2

We throw stuff away or we keep it in a hoard,
We buy it in the first place just because we were bored.
Some people say: "Gotta change our ways.
The earth is like an old man in his last days."

All: The earth is like an old man in his last days." x2

We all blame each other, and we say it with sorrow,
But we live as if there was no tomorrow.
Some people say that the future can be bright
We can all live well if we all live right.

All: We can all live well if we all live right. x2

Some people say it's too late to save the planet
Someone's already done it, the one who first began it.
Whatever you say – whatever you discover…
Be kind to the planet and be kind to one another…

All: Be kind to the planet and be kind to one another… x2

A Purple Patch

When any colour is mentioned point to that colour if you can see it
anywhere.

There was a **purple** man, lived in a **purple** land
With a **purple** wife and cat, **purple** house and welcome mat.
He bought a ticket one day, for the lottery to play
It wasn't **purple** though, but he was desperate to know
If his **purple** luck was in, if he might just win.

He picked six numbers with no link, wrote them all in **purple** ink,
Then watched on Saturday night, to see if he'd chosen right.
Well, as the lottery began there was a very loud bang!
The **purple** man saw **red** because his television set
Went all **green** and **yellow**, he was not a happy fellow,

He felt very **browned** off, though his wife just gave a cough.
She dragged him to the neighbours, and explained about his labours.
So they let the **Purples** in not believing they would win.
But from feeling rather **blue** the **Purples** turned a different hue.
Their luck had come around, they'd won ten million pound!

Now their neighbours turned bright **green** cause they hadn't won a bean.
The **purple** man scooped the lot and they'd not won a jot.
So they waited in a thicket till the man came with his ticket
To claim his **purple** win then they killed and buried him!
And when his **purple** wife came near they did the same to her!

And though it wasn't cricket they made off with the ticket,
Got the cash that day, and then tried to run away.
But the boys in **blue** were slick and they locked them in the nick.
So the moral of this mishap is that money is a big trap
It can help you when you're needy - it can also make you greedy.

The Good the Bad and the Cuddly

Chin – Rub chin thoughtfully
Jungle – Make jungle sounds, birds, lions, tigers, elephants, crickets
Desert – Wipe brow as if hot
Pyramids – Do an Egyptian sand dance
Mountain – Shiver and say "Brrr!"
Eagle – Put out arms like wings and glide from side to side, saying "Neeeyow!"

Little Dog Moffet had big brown eyes, a double **chin** and huge floppy ears. He also had a friend called Ragged Bone. Ragged Bone was smaller than Little Dog Moffet and he only had a single **chin**, not a double **chin**. Ragged Bone and Little Dog were very good friends and had been so for many years and many adventures.

One day they decided to go and look for heaven because they had a few questions for God. They caught a train, and then they caught a boat, then they got on a plane and then they got on a jeep and drove and drove and drove until they came to a **jungle**. They hacked their way through the **jungle**, past the palm trees and under the tall creepers, dodging the elephants and leaping the lions until they came to a **desert**. It was very hot and they rode on camels across the bright brown sand. They came to some **pyramids** and there they met a sharp nosed, long eared wolf called Stephen Sphinx. Little Dog asked him, "Is this where heaven is?"
But Stephen Sphinx shook his head, "This is the **pyramids**, they're full of old kings," he said.
"Perhaps they might know," said Ragged Bone, but Stephen Sphinx shook his head.
"They're not alive anymore," he said.
"Hmm," Little Dog Moffet scratched his double **chin** and Ragged Bone saw him do this so he scratched his single **chin** too.

They climbed back onto their camels, and Stephen Sphinx climbed on too and they left the **desert** and the **pyramids** and rode off into the sunset. After a while they came to a **mountain**.

Ragged Bone pointed up and said, "I bet if we climb this **mountain** it will take us up to heaven," so they got off their camels and started climbing. Soon it got very dark and the **mountain** became all snowy. Then suddenly a big white monster stepped out of the darkness and said, "Hello I'm Yolanda the Yeti, and I don't get many visitors. What are you doing here?" Yolanda was very big and snowy and she had a lot more **chins** than Little Dog or Ragged Bone. They told her they were looking for heaven and she said, "I'll come with you up to the top of the **mountain** to see if it's up there." On the way up she said, "D'you know the football results, because I'm a Liverpool fan and my television doesn't work properly up here." But Little Dog Moffet was an Everton fan, so he didn't take much notice of Liverpool.

At the top of the **mountain** they found a very old **eagle**. He had a wise grey head; a dusty old beak and he wore little brown sandals. He was sitting on a rock.

"Hello," said Little Dog Moffet, "is this heaven?"

The old **eagle** rubbed his **chin** with his wing and smiled.

"No," he said, "but you're very close."

"Where do we have to go then?" asked Ragged Bone. "We have some questions for God."

The **eagle** rubbed his **chin** again. "You don't have to go anywhere," he said, "just sit quietly, close your eyes and talk to God wherever you are."

"Can't we meet him though?" asked Yolanda the Yeti.

"Not yet," said the **eagle**, "but one day you will. You can talk to him now though, tell him about yourself, tell him your mistakes and your problems, and tell him you'd like to get to know him and see what happens. That's the only way I know to get to meet God."

"Suppose he doesn't like us," said Ragged Bone who was always a little worried that people wouldn't like him.

"Oh don't worry about that," said the **eagle**, "he likes everyone, the good, the bad and the cuddly."

And with that Little Dog Moffet, Ragged Bone, Stephen Sphinx and Yolanda the Yeti turned and went back down the **mountain**, back across the **desert**, back past the **pyramids**, back through the **jungle** and all the way back home.

Y2K

Car – "Vroom, vroom!"   Television **– "Turn it down!"**
Wii – Mime holding controls and playing games
Lottery - Rip ticket in half   **Popular** – Applause
Jokes – Laugh   **Powers** – "Zap!"   **Questions** – "Errr…" Scratch head

How long is a millennium? (*Look around and wait for someone to tell you*)
Yes, **1000 years**, so 1000 years ago it was the year… **1000**. That's right.
How long is a bi-millennium? **2000 years**, and so 2000 years ago it was…
right - zero. (*Adjust these figures depending on the actual year*)
In 1000 years from now it will be… (*Wait for guesses*) yes, the year **3000**,
and in 2000 years from now it will be… (*Wait*) yes, the year **4000**.
In 1000 years people might be living on the moon.
In 2000 years they might be living on Mars.
Not the chocolate – the planet. Some people already live on Mars Bars.
We've come a long way since 2000 years ago. Now we've got the **car**, the
television, the **Wii** and the **lottery**.
Back in the year zero they didn't have the **car**, the **television**, the **Wii** or
the **lottery**.
But there's one thing that was very different back then. 2000 years ago
something much more amazing than the **car**, the **television**, the **Wii** or the
lottery arrived on this planet.
About 2000 years ago a tiny baby was born… And that's what started the
millennium clock ticking.
You see, this baby was so amazing that people started counting time from
the year he was born.
So the year 2000 meant it was 2000 years since the birth of a tiny baby
boy, in a place called Bethlehem in a country called Israel.
There were lots of babies born 2000 years ago – so I wonder why we
celebrate the birth of this one?
Was it because he was **popular**?
Was it because he told stories and **jokes**?
Was it because he had special **powers**?
Was it because he could answer any **question**?
Actually it was because he was an amazing person who changed history
and changed our planet forever.

19979370R00133

Printed in Great Britain
by Amazon